# CHARGE UP YOUR BUSINESS!

## 27 Ways to Boost Profits

Giorgio Bicego, B.A.Sc., P.Eng.
Multiple Award Winning Author
www.chargeupyourbusinessbook.com
www.gbicego.com

Publisher
10-10-10 Publishing
Markham, ON  Canada
Printed in the United States of America
ISBN: 978-1-77277-127-5
ebook: 978-1-77277-145-9

# Contents

# DEDICATION

*I dedicate this book to my parents Gianfranco and Vittoria who took a chance to immigrate to Canada to make a better life for themselves, our families, and for generations to come. Thank you for your love, sacrifices, hard work, support, and for setting an example for all of us.*

# TESTIMONIALS

Giorgio has expanded company sales, improved cost structures, and increased business profits up to millions of dollars – he is professional, hard-working, and committed to delivering results.
**Gianzo Mastrangelo, Vice President Sales – Brampton, ON**

Giorgio identified improvement ideas within his first few days, further assessed our business needs, and then implemented initiatives, saving hundreds of thousands of dollars every year.
**Robert Wallace, Plant Manager – Fergus, ON**

Giorgio led our operations group, helping improve our employee safety, product/process quality, and productivity while improving OEEs (overall equipment effectiveness) by 15%+.
**Stuart Faria, Plant Manager – Brampton, ON**

Giorgio has extensive knowledge in the field of program management, ranging from quoting, driving formal business awards, commercial negotiations, supplier sourcing/purchasing, and liaising with both suppliers and customers while launching programs/processes on-time and on-budget.
**Craig Clute, Program Manager – Newmarket, ON**

Giorgio is a fantastic leader who is energetic, driven, and passionate in whatever he does; he is one of the best people I've ever worked for and always ensured we met our customer delivery requirements.
**Gwen Crampton, Demand Planning – ERP Specialist – Toronto, ON**

Giorgio is one of the most effective leaders I know; he is emotionally intelligent, wise, and a "people person" leader who guides and works well with all types of people while excelling in a wide variety of situations.
**Aklilu Zere, Machine Division Manager – Etobicoke, ON**

# ACKNOWLEDGEMENTS

This book is a reflection in many ways of who I am and how I think in some areas of my life. Therefore, I first acknowledge my parents, Gianfranco and Vittoria, for immigrating to Canada and providing me an opportunity for a better life, and for loving and supporting me every step of the way. I also acknowledge my three sons—Étienne, François, and Alexandre—who mean the most to me and who I will always love much more than you know. I have always been, am, and will be, very proud of each and every one of you as you continue your own life journeys. I acknowledge my Liz who shares my life and whose love and support helps define me as the person I am and am becoming. I value my sister, Lisa, and her family, as well as all my cousins, aunts, and uncles, and long-time friends—Gianzo, Sebastijan, Frank, Tony, Anthony, Stuart, and others—who have always been with me throughout the good and the more challenging times.

I acknowledge and value my clients whom I've had the privilege of serving and helping with their businesses and lives. I thank my past employers who gave me an opportunity to support myself and family, and I acknowledge former work colleagues—Tom, Joseph, Richard, Ed, Hans, Glen, Carlo, Carolyn, Terry, Frank, Ana, Craig, Aklilu, Gwen, and Rob—who I now call friends.

I thank my coaches and mentors, Raymond Aaron, James Allen, Sir Richard Branson, Dr. Wayne Dyer, Napoleon Hill, Jim Rohn, Tony Robbins, and Oprah Winfrey. I also thank teachers from throughout my formal education—Mrs. Schweinberger, Mr. Vella, Mr. Hebor and Mr. Pascale—who taught me life lessons not included in their standard course curriculums.

I value and want to thank the people at The Raymond Aaron Group— Liz, Carla, Christina (for your help with the media kit and website), Rosa (for your extraordinary help as my book architect, answering my questions, and guiding me through this book writing journey), Helen and Mikee—and at 10-10-10 Publishing, who helped me put together and publish this book. A special thank you to Lisa who edited my books and makes my writing look great!

I apologize if I am forgetting anyone.

Finally, I acknowledge and thank you who have entrusted me with your time to read this book. I am humbled and grateful for the opportunity to share my ideas with you. Please contact me at www.chargeupyourbusinessbook.com and/or www.gbicego.com with your feedback, or to find out how I can help you and your business achieve your goals.

# FOREWORD

I have known Giorgio Bicego for over thirty years, and was thrilled when he decided to author his first book, *Charge Up Your Business!: 27 Ways to Boost Profits*. By reading Giorgio's book, you will gain design solutions and insight for your business challenges, while implementing strategies to help you achieve your business goals. Giorgio shares some of his personal business experiences as examples, to reaffirm that his concepts and approaches will work for you and your organization.

In *Charge Up Your Business!*, Giorgio will teach you that you must address your finances, operations, and continuous improvement initiatives when leading or working in a successful business. Giorgio is honest, professional, and straightforward, and you will see this reflected in the lessons he teaches you within this book.

After reading *Charge Up Your Business!*, I am certain that you will discover new ideas, and perhaps be reminded of other strategies that will help you boost your business profits. Contact Giorgio to help you achieve your business goals today!

Raymond Aaron
New York Times Bestselling Author

# INTRODUCTION

Hello! Thank you for purchasing and reading this book! I wrote this book to offer my best advice and experiences in leading and working in successful businesses within several industries and throughout various parts of the world. As I began documenting my ideas and experiences in my original work, it became apparent that my manuscript was growing beyond my intentions in subjects and size. I also noticed my ideas supported two dominant themes I recommend and have always believed are necessary to lead any successful business: the science of running an organization (the mechanics of finance, operations, and continuous improvements), and the art of leadership and working with people (how to maximize your peoples' performances).

After considering advice from trusted friends and advisers, I decided to separate my original work into two books, each uniquely dedicated to focusing on the science of business and the art of leadership. I believe each of these two themes are so important, they deserve their own distinct book. The title of my other book is *Charge Up Your People!: 27 Ways to Boost Performance* (www.chargeupyour peoplebook.com). You may consider the science of business as the foundation for your company operations and the art of leadership and working with people as the fuel that will propel your organization to achieve its goals.

This book is about the science of running your business, focusing on your finances, operations, and continuous improvements. As with many strong entities found in nature and human design, I suggest you need to master all these three areas to run your successful business. Your finances consist at minimum of your business plan, budget(s), and cash flow activities—these are crucial requirements to plan and administer your business. Running your operations can be simplified by focusing and prioritizing your efforts in safety, quality, business systems, production, maintenance, and security. And your continuous improvement activities will allow you and your team(s) to drive your business efficiencies and improve your profits.

This book is written for you who currently leads or plans to lead/run, improve, and work within a successful business. I present many ideas and insights to improve your organization and avoid potential catastrophes. Along the way, I have included my own personal business experiences highlighting various concepts. These ideas may be considered for your business regardless if you lead yourself, a small group, or large international groups of people striving to provide a product and/or service to your targeted market place(s).

Please send me your testimonials about this book and the ideas and concepts contained within. I always welcome your feedback of how these ideas and concepts have helped you and/or your business.

In the end, I cannot possibly anticipate and provide solutions in this book for every potential challenge faced by you and your business. I invite you to contact us at www.chargeupyourbusinessbook.com and/or www.gbicego.com if you would like more information and advice for your challenge(s) and how we can help you and your business achieve your goals and objectives.

# PART I – YOUR FINANCES

# CHAPTER 1

# YOUR FINANCIALS

## Business Plan

Congratulations! You have decided to start your own business! Or perhaps you've been asked to start a new venture with an existing company, or take charge of a division(s) within your current organization! That's fantastic! After your initial euphoria and excitement, the questions start: "How do I start?" "When do I start?" "Do I need new employees or keep the current employees?" "Where do I do my business?" "Do I need any start-up or more funds?" "What are my start-up or current expenses?" "How long will it take to get going?" You may consider avoiding these questions and jump right in and develop your business plan on the fly—you won't be the first or the last person to try this strategy. And you may hear stories of the odd time when such a *shot gun* approach turned out well for a now well-known business leader. But I suggest a well thought out and documented business plan is a prudent way to start developing or taking over a business without assuming too many unnecessary risks.

Starting your new business, or taking over a current business, is risky—you know that. Risk is not bad, of course, but why not minimize your risks as much as you can by completing your business plan? I suggest that's one of the most important purposes for your business plan: mitigating your risks. You may find that the process of developing a documented business plan compels you to clarify your business ideas and acts as an important feasibility test of those ideas. Who knows, perhaps you may find a fundamental flaw(s) with your assessment—which I think is fantastic at this stage – before you've invested significant time and financial resources. Perhaps as you progress through your business plan process, you will identify other challenges and their solutions that you may not have thought of earlier. Again, this is a great opportunity to identify any and all potential issues and design plans to meet those challenges before investing any significant time and financial resources.

Your business plan is most likely the first or one of the first few documents you complete when starting your new business or taking over an existing business, especially if you are planning to ask people to invest their money and time into your company. I've seen the beginnings of business plans take shape from notes on restaurant napkins, miscellaneous pieces of paper, easels, white boards, post it notes, all the way to extensive documents with appendices and graphs. Your business plan is unique to you and your business, and should serve you and any other parties as required. Therefore, I recommend you use a business plan format that meets your own and your audience's needs.

Despite of what form your business plan takes, I suggest it should include most or all of these sections: an executive summary (especially if you're presenting your business plan to an audience), your goals, a SWOT analysis, a marketing and sales plan, financial plan, business structure, operations plans, and timelines. I briefly describe each of your business plan sections below.

I recommend that you must include an executive summary in your business plan if you are submitting it to anyone for financing purposes. Your executive summary is typically a brief description of your business, its purpose and goals, structure, and projected cash flow. Typically, your executive summary is less than a page long and should recap your financing requirements.

Your next business plan section describes your goals and how you plan to achieve those objectives. This section is critical as it summarizes why you are in business. Typically, you include how your product and/or service will fill a market niche(s) in their own unique manner(s). Your sales, income, and other financial goals are also normally included in this section.

Your SWOT analysis is perhaps the most critical element of your business plan. SWOT stands for Strengths, Weaknesses, Opportunities, and Threats. In this exercise, you first identify your business strengths that you will use to achieve your objectives. Your business strengths can be your own personal characteristics and/or of others involved in your business, the unique capabilities of your products and/or services, etc. I suggest you do not be humble at this point—list any and all your strengths here. Next step is to identify any business weaknesses; similar to your strengths, these weaknesses can be your personal ones and any within your business product and/or service. Then, list all the opportunities that exist within your business and marketplace(s). This third step may seem easier than the others since it's those opportunities that first grabbed your attention, causing you to think about starting your new business or taking over an existing business in the first place. Finally, document any threats to your business; these may range from competitors (both potential and current) within your marketplace(s) and/or any other local, national, or international issues that may affect your business and customers. A SWOT analysis is perhaps one of the most critical activities when developing your business plan and may take up to a day, days, or even longer to develop. I suggest you give your SWOT analysis the serious attention it deserves. As a result of your SWOT analysis process, you may want to reassess your business goals and other parts of your business plan. I have led and witnessed instances where businesses actually changed their main objectives or added other *sub-businesses* to their portfolio as results of a well-run SWOT exercise.

Fresh from completing your SWOT analysis, your marketing and sales plan then addresses how you will reach your target market(s) and sell to your customers. You may want to include results of your own market analyses, detailing how large your market is or will be, and how you will attract and deliver your product and/or service to your customers. You may want to emphasize some of your SWOT analysis strength and opportunities if you are submitting your business plan to convince your audience that your company truly has unique abilities to fulfill your customers' needs. You may also want to address any weaknesses or threats you identified during your SWOT analysis in this section. Pricing points and strategies are also usually included in this section after showing the value that you will provide to your customers. You can describe how your business will reach its customers through various marketing strategies and then describe how it plans to deliver your product and/or service to your market place(s). You may describe how your business requires something as simple as a website, a small office, an industrial unit, or an entire building(s) to deliver your product and/or service.

Your financial plan should, at minimum, include your start up and operations budgets, detailing any one-time set-up and on-going expenses. Also recommended are your income and cash flow projections to give yourself, and your audience if necessary, details on what sales revenues your business will generate to cover your expenses. Normally, a projected balance sheet(s) will complete the minimum financial documents included in this section. I recommend you will need to produce very detailed financial documents for yourself, and then you may want to present summaries of these financial documents in your business plan, especially if you are submitting it to someone for financing purposes.

Your next step is to outline your business structure. In this section, I suggest you describe what your business will look like and how it will function. In the case of your new business, or if you are taking over an existing one, I suggest the following questions will help you design your new structure, or redesign your current structure: What legal form will your business take? Where will you conduct your business? Do you need an office, a building(s), or can you just run it on-line, out of your own home for now? Do you need a separate website(s), business phone number(s), separate bank accounts, etc.? Do you need any partners or any employees, and, if so, how many and when do you need them? What will their job descriptions be, to whom will they report to, and will they have anyone reporting to them? Then, I suggest you describe the process of providing your product(s) and/or service(s), and what equipment you may need, if any, to deliver them to your customers.

Following your business structure section, your business plan should outline your operations plan(s). Your overall operations plan may consist of *sub-plans* addressing your goals and objectives for health & safety, the environment, quality, and production. You may also consider including information detailing your maintenance, business systems, and security priorities as well.

Finally, I suggest you develop a timeline(s) detailing what will happen by when, and who will be responsible to complete each task. If you're applying for a business loan to start your new business, or to inject additional capital into your current business, I recommend specifying how much money will be required at each major event. It is important to be realistic with your tasks and target dates.

As a final note, I advise that your business plan should be a *live* document, i.e. reviewed and updated on a regular basis. At first, you may need to do this on a daily or weekly basis as your new business lifts off the ground. As you grow your new business or progress within your existing one, I suggest you review your business plan on a monthly, quarterly, or, at least, annual basis. I find reviewing my business plans on a regular basis keeps me focused on my short and long term objectives and my progress to achieve them.

## Budget(s)

Your budget and related income statement are two of your most important business and financial documents. Typically, when people think of a *budget*, they may immediately think of their business expenses, but there obviously is also a *sales budget* for any business venture. I recommend your overall budget reflects all major items in your income statement and may be comprised of several *mini budgets* such as a sales budget, capital expenditures, materials, labour, overhead expenses, etc. It is critical to include every single type of revenue and expense in your budgets. If it's not your first year in business, the easiest and most obvious way to develop next year's budget is based on this and/or last year's budget. But I caution that some item(s) may have been missed in this and/or last year's budget, so I recommend you also review this and/or last year's list of general ledger accounts. I furthermore suggest you consider that your business may change in the coming year, thus incurring new types of revenues and/or expenses.

Who should develop your budgets? If you have a controller and/or accountant, most likely they will be put in charge of developing your budgets and other financial documents. I suggest one of the worst things you can do when developing a budget is developing it entirely on your own. Even if you're a sole proprietor with no employees, I advise you get other opinions about your projected income statement and budgets. Especially if you have employees that may be responsible for aspects of your business financial performance, I suggest one of the worst things you can do is exclusively develop the budget(s) yourself and then delegate the numbers and expectations to your employees. I advise you may find it more difficult trying to hold your employees accountable to meet budget numbers that only you developed for them without their participation. If you have other employees reporting to you, I advise that you ask them to develop their own department budget(s) to provide them an opportunity to be more engaged in the business. In some cases, as appropriate, the extent to which your employees surpass their budget targets may be part of their personal or department compensation package(s). As soon as all department budget(s) are drafted, submitted, and combined into an overall business budget, you may find all-too-familiar negotiations ensue as the department heads may ask to spend more, while their superior replies they need to spend less. I suggest these discussions are beneficial for both parties since they provide an opportunity for each person to learn about aspects of the business from a different viewpoint.

Once your overall budget is developed and finalized, I suggest you conduct a sensitivity or *stress* test by decreasing sales by 15% or so and leaving the expenses the same or increasing them by 15% or so. If you still break even or meet minimum expected profitability, that's great! If you don't, you may have more work to do. I suggest you consider following this rule of budgeting: if your budget and projected profits remain acceptable after reducing sales revenue by 15% and increasing expenses by 15%, it's a good budget.

I also strongly recommend monitoring your income(s) and expenses regularly - at least every two weeks or every month as a minimum. I also advise, if feasible, that you have your controller present weekly and month-to-date revenue and expenses updates and to forecast the remaining of the current month and your next three rolling months' revenues and expenses. I suggest conducting these pre-emptive weekly reviews to detect and begin fixing any developing negative trends before month end. In addition, I recommend always conducting a *budget* vs. *actual* analysis on both sales and expense budgets, and discussing the findings with any employees involved in those processes—you may also find it useful to complete this exercise for every large project. I suggest this exercise represents another opportunity to engage your employees in the *mechanics* of running and working within the business, and is beneficial for all parties.

After some time and experience, you may be able to personally *sense* what is going on and how well your business is doing financially. Regardless, I suggest it is always more prudent to act proactively, especially when dealing with your business finances.

## Cash Flow

What is the *lifeblood* of your business? Your product(s)? Your service(s)? Your customers? Referrals? Your employees? Or your suppliers? Yes, I agree all these people and things are required for your business to *exist*, even for a short while, but I suggest your business requires a steady positive cash flow to *thrive*. You may have heard of the saying "cash is king." I believe that for any business, "cash *flow* is king" or "cash *flow* is queen," if you'd like; I suggest this statement is a universal business law that is inescapable, just like gravity. You may also have heard of another quote: "In this world, nothing can be said to be certain except death and taxes." Just as I suggest death is the only true certainty in life, "cash *flow* is king/queen" is the only inescapable certainty for your business survival and growth. If you need more convincing about this concept, you may want to research the top reasons why most businesses collapse. You may find one of the top reasons for most business failures is financial mismanagement, or they run out of money; the reason(s) why they run out of money may vary, but in the end every insolvent business fails. So, that's why, in every business I run (and I suggest you do the same for yours), I personally and regularly monitor cash flow amongst other leading indicators—I recommend that you never forget to do so.

I advise that one of the best strategies to monitor and manage your cash flow is to track your accounts receivables and payables on a regular basis. I suggest you do so on a weekly basis and, if feasible, assign one or two people to track both accounts receivables and payables, and produce a report for your review. For accounts receivable, I suggest you setup a process to monitor their status as current, 30, 45, 60, 75, and 90+ days overdue. I recommend that you assign someone who will follow-up with all outstanding accounts receivable on a regular basis and track all commitments and dates in a report. If any of those interactions trigger any alarms or raise any flags, then I suggest you have the issue escalated to that person's supervisor/manager, then to finance, and then to the sales person and/or their manager. For accounts payable, your finance person and/or department can generate a schedule of payments that must be maintained so your business can remain current with your suppliers. Depending on your business structure and the amount of receivables in question, you may find it necessary that you yourself may need to get involved to resolve any issue(s).

I recall one situation when I assumed responsibility over a product line. I viewed it as a simple business although we produced somewhat technically advanced products comprised of many intricate components and processes. I quickly conducted investigations about the status of our deliveries, any supplier and quality concerns, and set up weekly update meetings to track these issues. I also discovered one of our main customers had not paid us in months. At first it was difficult for me to believe this fact; perhaps this was one of the reasons I was assigned as the new business manager for this product line. We began addressing our customer late payment issues with our accounting people communicating with their accounting people. Eventually, I needed to get personally involved due to the very large amount of monies owed to our company. After several attempts and broken promises to have this issue resolved, I implemented an extreme measure of sending our customer a "pay us, or we no longer ship" letter. This action and type of letter may seem risky, and I suggest it should be considered as a last resort, but it proved to be effective in this case. Within two days of sending this "pay us, or we no longer ship" letter, I drove to our customer's facility to receive a cheque for a large amount representing the majority of our past due accounts receivable with them. I am also glad to report that our customer then continued to pay our company on time after this incident.

After everything is said and done, I recommend you always ensure no one fools around or plays games with your cash flow. As I've already stated, I advise your cash flow is the life blood of your business, and recommend you always watch your cash flow like a hawk.

## For More Information and Advice

Please contact us at www.chargeupyourbusinessbook.com and/or www.gbicego.com if you would like more information about, and advice for, your financial challenges such as your business plan, budget(s), cash flow and/or any other challenges—we are here to help.

# CHAPTER 2

# QUOTING, COSTING & PRICING

## The Importance of Quoting, Costing & Pricing

I suggest your quoting strategies and methods play a very crucial part in determining your business financial success. Accepting a badly quoted order(s), even once depending on its enormity and impact, may result in potential business catastrophes unless you're running an organization where you or the owner(s) does not mind regularly pouring in capital to finance any business loss(es). Your costing methods are critical to your business's financial success since your profits are the result of your revenues minus costs. You may be amazed how often this simple *profit equals revenues minus costs* concept is ignored at times during some business sales negotiations and conversations.

I have thus far developed, improved, and used various quoting/costing models for over twenty-five years, and not one of them are similar in format since they are used to quote and cost their respective unique products and services. It is important to include all design, development, manufacturing, delivery processes, and related costs in your quote/cost model. I have found that many or all quoting/ costing models share common elements such as materials, labour and benefits, purchased parts, equipment, tooling, freight, packaging, overheads (both fixed and variable), consumables, and SG&A (Selling, General and Administrative) costs. One area where quoting/cost spreadsheets share both common and unique characteristics is overhead cost allocation. I strongly recommend that your business always follows GAAP (Generally Accepted Accounting Practices) when allocating overhead costs and completing all financial tasks and reports.

## Quoting Strategies

I was once told by a colleague that their business mentor once told them, "If you want to make money in this business, you're going to have to become a liar!" Now, of course, I do not accept or support lying in any form, but you may understand the point that mentor was trying to make with this statement. I suggest the basis for your entire business, and every quote, is the financial difference between the value placed by your customer(s) on your product(s) and/or service(s), typically reflected in your sales prices or revenues, and your total internal costs. I assume one of your main business objectives, if not "the" main objective, is to generate profits; i.e. ensure your external customer revenues consistently exceed your internal costs, unless you are leading or in a non-profit organization.

I suggest every effective quote model and each one of its items be structured or divided into *two halves* or have *two numbers*: your external customer price and its related internal cost. The combined competitiveness of your overall external customer price and your related internal cost will hopefully result in a business profit or at least break-even situation. For example, if your actual labour cost including benefits may be $1.00, you may decide to charge your customer $1.50—the difference is what you call *profit*. I apologise if I seem to be "stating the obvious," but again you may be amazed how often this simple *profit equals revenues minus costs* concept is ignored at times by people engaged in business activities. I advise that you avoid accepting anyone's statement or accusation that you may be lying to your customer(s) if you find yourself trying to justify your prices and/or this concept of your *two numbers* quote model structure. In my opinion, such a person either doesn't understand how business works and/or may be an employee who should be content your business pays their wage.

There are generally two quoting methods: I call them the *ground up* and the *drive down* approaches. The first and more popular *ground up* method consists of building up your final sales price by first determining your actual materials, labour, and overhead costs, and then adding a markup(s) to reach a final price that will hopefully be attractive to your customer(s). The second method, the *drive down* approach, begins with a competitive market price that your customer(s) is willing to pay, and then you subtract your basic materials, labour, and overhead costs to hopefully result in a profit. Both *ground up* and *drive down* approaches are effective quoting methods; choosing which approach works best for you and your business depends on your market and personal preference.

You may be asking yourself, "Who should complete my business quotes?" If you're on your own in business, the answer is simple: you are the person completing all your quotes as you do with many other tasks. But what if you are leading a larger business with other employees and functions? One answer is to have your controller or finance people complete all the quotes since they should know all your costs. This strategy may sound logical, but you may find your controller and finance employees are either too busy completing other critical tasks or may tend to be too conservative and over-estimate your business costs to a point that your quotes are uncompetitive. Another answer is to delegate all quoting activities to your sales people since they should know best what your customer(s) are willing to pay and are looking for. I propose the challenge with this strategy is that some sales people may be too aggressive in order to get the sale to perhaps meet their own objectives and/or to meet your overall business objectives.

My advice is you consider selecting and training someone from your business operations area to *spearhead* or lead all your quote activities, thus avoiding anyone from your finance or sale function(s), for two main reasons. The first reason is that your operations people typically know more about how to develop your service(s) and/or manufacture your product(s) than anyone else in your business. The second reason is that your operations people will be denied any excuse that they were not involved in the quoting process if they encounter issues when completing your product and/or service delivery process. Your quoting person(s) must be detail oriented, disciplined, and never forget any step in the established quoting process, regardless of who you choose to complete your quoting activities. It may also be necessary that quoting work be completed in a quiet place and in a focused manner to avoid mistakes. I also recommend your quoting person(s) be located close to any existing similar process(es) in case they may want to investigate any current or new potential issue(s). You may also consider establishing a quoting department or process consisting of a group of employees, each performing specific tasks such as collecting supplier quotes to actually producing the quote(s) themselves.

Your quoting/cost model format can be as varied as the person who spearheads your quoting activities. I have seen everything from more complicated databases and server-based software programs where you enter data to generate what seems to be an endless number of quote scenarios and analyses, to a simple *back of a restaurant napkin* quick quote calculation. Once again, I recommend you use whatever quote model format that makes sense for your business. You may consider, as I prefer, using a Microsoft Excel spreadsheet(s) as the basis for all your quotes, for several reasons such as ease of construction, ease of naming quote spreadsheet files and filing them in an appropriate directory, flexibility to make changes/improvements, and to quickly and easily analyze varying scenarios. For example, with Microsoft Excel, you can place two spreadsheets side by side with different selling prices and margins to review different product and/or service development or manufacturing methods. You may also use a Microsoft Excel quote spreadsheet to *reverse* engineer what margin and/or cost levels would have been required to match a customer's target price or someone else's winning bid price. Although they may not need to be an *Excel Master* to effectively use Microsoft Excel as your quoting platform, your quoting person(s) may require additional training to take advantage of its features to design and employ more effective quote spreadsheets to meet your business needs.

Regardless of who generates your business quotes and how they are structured, I suggest you consider at least engaging a group of individuals represented by various areas of your business such as sales, finance, and operations to review all quotes before submitting them to your customers. You may also consider personally reviewing all quotes or advising your *quoting group,* after you've established certain criteria, to contact you for a personal review of specific business quotes before their submission. I also recommend that you are at least advised of all quotes being sent to customers.

As a final thought about quoting, you may wonder what you do if your potential or current customer(s) asks for a quoted sales price/cost breakdown. In fact, your customer(s) may even require you submit a sales price/cost breakdown with every quote. First of all, I suggest you assess the importance of any price/cost breakdown to your customer(s), and your chance(s) of obtaining new business and/or maintaining current business with them. My advice is two-fold: my first piece of advice is to never submit any sales price/cost breakdown with any of your company's quotes for any reason(s). My advice is to first reply that your company quote sales price/cost breakdowns are private and confidential, proprietary to your business, and generally not available. I suggest you consider that submitting any price/ cost breakdown may provide a free insight into your business financials, not only to your customer but to anyone else they may share this information with, even once. In fact, you may have experienced (as have I) that some customers may ask you to *open your books* to assure themselves your business is financially viable. Although there may be some truth to this statement, I suggest there may be other hidden reasons for this request. I also caution you that as your company submits price/cost breakdowns to any particular customer over time, their own people may begin to develop their own database of your quoted prices and costs. But if you must submit a sales price/cost breakdown with your quote(s), my second piece of advice is to do so strategically and with great care, being mindful of the potential and very real consequences. And, of course, if you need to submit any quote/sales price/cost breakdown, I advise you submit only your quote model *customer* numbers.

I suggest there are two critical pieces of information required for any worthwhile quoting exercise: an accurate determination of your internal costs, and a realistic assessment of what price(s) your customers will accept. I discuss both these key quoting requirements in the following sections.

## Costing Strategies

The first of the two critical keys to effective quoting is to know your costs very well. I suggest too many companies have almost or eventually gone bankrupt due to accepting a job(s) that was priced too low and/or below their inaccurate cost estimates. Your business may be able to survive if you underestimated your costs for a smaller value quote. I suggest that prolonged use of underestimated cost estimates in your quotes will eventually result in your business failure, unless you, your owner, or financial institution don't mind financing your operational losses. I advise your costing accuracy is crucial to your business financial success because it forms the basis for the *ground up* quoting method and will accurately tell you if you will make a profit when using the *drive down* quoting approach.

You may be wondering how to obtain an accurate evaluation and knowledge of your costs. The answer is quite simple and its wording may seem similar to the question: ensure you determine all your costs as accurately as possible! I recommend you review every type of business expense and ensure it is considered into your quote/cost model as appropriate. If you find it necessary, you may find it advantageous to hire a consultant and/or cost accountant on a contract or full-time basis to determine, maintain, and regularly review all your costing information accuracy.

Although it may be practically impossible to list all your quote model costing items, here are some obvious costs to consider when quoting: design and development, raw materials, components, and any scrap produced during processing and setups. There are also direct and indirect labour costs, consumable items during processing and setups, packaging (either one-time or reusable), and delivery/ freight costs associated with your outgoing product and/or service, incoming components and/or raw material(s). I recommend you do not forget any engineering and/or testing costs, and other overhead costs such as equipment capital costs, floor space, and/or facility costs. The composition of your quote model cost items list will be as unique as your business process(es), and your overall costing accuracy is determined by the degrees to which your cost item list contains each and every business expense item, and the accuracy of each item.

Another important strategy I recommend to ensure accurate costing (and thus quoting) is to conduct a *quote versus budget* or *quote versus actual* analysis, where you literally compare actual or budgeted costs to your quoted costs. This *acid* test exercise will also reveal your actual profit (or loss) compared to what you forecasted at the time when your quote was submitted to and accepted by your customer(s). I advise you complete this analysis sometime after your process has achieved *steady state* when most/all issues have been resolved during the job launch phase. I have always used, and suggest you also use, this exercise to continue *tweaking* or modifying your quoting/cost model until your *quoted* costs are within a reasonable difference of your actual costs for any particular group of products and/or services. I suggest you can remain confident that your overall costing methods and structure are accurate and reliable after you have achieved your costing accuracy goals and as long as you continue to follow every step in your quoting model/process. Even if you strategically decide to submit a price resulting in a forecasted break-even or loss, at least you will know that fact before you submit your bid. I propose one of the worst things affecting your business's survival and growth is to be awarded and accept a job with an anticipated profit only to find out later by surprise that you are actually losing money.

After successive and favorable *quote versus budget* or *quote versus actual* reviews, you and your employees may be able to develop rules to at least quickly cost/quote any product and/or service to any customer at any time. Your *fast quote* process involves estimating or confirming a single piece or a few critical pieces of data and multiplying them by a factor(s) to develop a *safe quote* on the spot, if required to keep a potential customer interested in your business. I strongly advise, though, to be very careful if a potential customer asks you for a fast bid on the spot, and to assess your realistic chances of obtaining new business if you do so. Perhaps you may want to prequalify your *fast quote* as an estimate just in case you may have overlooked, and/or had not been given, all the opportunity details at that time. I recall an occasion when I was asked to *fast quote* an item in a customer's office. Although I reached a point where I developed an accurate costing model and was obviously aware of our expected margins to *fast quote* this item, I resisted the temptation to do so and replied that I would quickly submit a bid once I received more details.

## Pricing Strategies

The second of the two critical keys to effective quoting is to know what price(s) your customers are willing to pay. How many times have you heard a statement like: "Only three things matter to obtain new business or keep current business—price, price, and price!" If price is the only significant determining factor to obtain new business, good luck because you may be in a commodity market. It's not impossible to make money in a commodity market, but just be aware that your business competitiveness may/will be driven to some/a large extent by forces external to your business product and/or service. I suggest almost any market can be thought of as a commodity market to some degree because price is usually considered in any purchasing decision, unless you are in a *money is no object* kind of marketplace. In addition to a competitive price, I advise you ensure every customer acknowledges that your company also offers other advantages such as quality, service, support, and other user-friendly benefits. I suggest the likelihood of increasing your price(s) is directly dependent on how unique your non-price benefits are to your customers.

In addition to price and other benefits, I recommend you consider using mutually favourable terms to both your company and your customer(s) to win business. When faced with similar prices, you may find your customer(s) will select your quote that offers them more favourable terms. You may be able to use a combination of price, benefits and terms to your business's favour depending on your business objectives. For example, you may find it advantageous to "give away" your product(s) and/or service(s) to your customer(s) for free, but then generate your business revenues from an on-going maintenance contract(s).

I propose your realistic assessment of both your market needs and your corresponding quoting strategies may vary on a case by case basis to achieve both your short and long term business goals. For example, you may want to bid low to break into a market or, on the other hand, bid too high just to dissuade unwanted business (if you're so lucky to be in such a position). You may also consider your timing of submitting a quote(s) as a means to achieve other business objectives. For example, submitting a quote right away may emphasize your quick business responsiveness and/or eagerness to obtain the job(s). On the other hand, you may elect to submit your quote at the last minute to prevent customers from *shopping around* your price and/or terms.

You may also consider varying your price, e.g. you may want to offer a discounted price to a distributor versus a *non-distributor* potential customer.

You may find yourself in a situation, more than you'd like to admit, where your business is up against a realistic or sometimes unrealistic low price from a competitor(s). What do you do? Do you match their lower price or perhaps submit an even lower one to get the business, or just walk away? Some sales people may be tempted to get such business at any "reasonable" cost. As a business owner and/or leader, you may at times be faced with the decision to either lower your price to get the job(s), with a lower margin and/or loss and keep your people employed, or keep your price as is and not get the job, and possibly have to lay off your employees. It's a tough decision. Depending on your business, you may be able to occasionally sustain and/or it may be necessary to accept a *loss leader* job to break into a market, but I recommend you remain aware that your business may not sustain such jobs without outside capital infusions. Sometimes it may seem you and your competitors are playing a game of chicken to see who is willing to lose the most money.

In my opinion, this *game of chicken* or *race to the bottom* of outbidding your competition with too-low pricing may be very dangerous for your business. Unless driven by extenuating circumstances, I advise you, as I have in the past, consider declining such quoting opportunities. I also suggest you consider avoiding a serious price bidding war where you and your competitors participate in a *price race to the bottom* because that's where your business may eventually end up—at the bottom of the ocean, below the break-even surface. I have always run my businesses with the philosophy—and suggest you consider a similar philosophy—that it is better at times to run a business at less-than-full capacity, with more flexibility, that may make some money or break-even while being available for another chance(s) to make more money at a later date. This situation is contrary to accepting too many orders at low, no, or negative margins, and running your company at or over capacity while accepting less business flexibility, typically overflowing with costs and perhaps business losses. It's your choice.

## Supplier Selection & Purchasing

I advise you consider your suppliers are almost as important to your business success as your employees, and perhaps more important in some ways than some of your customers. In my opinion, you can always find new customers, but finding and keeping the right employees and suppliers are critical to your business success. Unless your business is a *one-person show,* and you think you may not need anyone else's help or input to conduct your business, I suggest you will need suppliers. I propose suppliers are an extension of your business similar to your employees, and I advise you should always seek out, work with, and retain the best suppliers possible. In short, I suggest suppliers can make or break your business, similar to your employees. Based on these ideas, I propose supplier selection and purchasing play an important part of your quoting, costing, and pricing strategies, and to your business in general.

So, where do you find great suppliers? To find great employees, you have the option to seek out and use the services of an employment recruiter. Similar to finding great people, I recommend you ask other trusted suppliers, employees, and friends. If all else fails, you can expand your search for suppliers by networking at trade shows, searching the internet, or contacting various organizations. Depending on what product and/or service you are looking for, you may need to invest quite some time to find a suitable potential supplier. I recall one occasion when I spent weeks on the phone and internet searching for a supplier for a very important project. I started contacting people in North America in the morning, then shifted to Europe in the afternoon, and onto East Asia in the evening. I repeated these actions all day, every day, for a couple of weeks, until I finally found a supplier back in North America. Like finding great employees, you may find it is worth the time and effort to find great suppliers.

Once you have found more than one potential supplier for a particular product and/or service, how do you select the *right one* for your business? Similar to quoting, there seems to be too many people who say the three most important things to consider when selecting a supplier are: price, price, and price. And then, perhaps, quality is important too, as an afterthought. I propose this typical method of selecting suppliers solely or mainly based on price is full of risks and potential problems for your business. How many times have you experienced, or have heard of another's experience, where they sourced the supplier with the cheapest price and then regretted doing so? It seems, at times, there is never enough money at the beginning of a project to do a job right the first time, but then there always seems to be more money in the middle or at the end of a project to fix what could have been avoided if you spent a little bit more money at the beginning. Despite what potential suppliers may tell and/or promise you, I suggest there is a universal law of sourcing products and services that works in every situation, in any language, anywhere in the world: you get what you pay for! As the saying goes, "If it sounds too good to be true, it probably is!"

I recommend the best method to source suppliers is using a *purchasing decision matrix.* A purchasing decision matrix is designed by generating a supplier selection criteria list, assigning a weighting to each selection criteria, and then ranking each potential supplier for each criteria. Some potential supplier selection criteria items are: quality, price, terms, freight, warranty, location (i.e. proximity to your business), and currency (used to purchase their product and/or service). I recommend you also consider listing and using other selection criteria such as annual maintenance costs (if any), ease of maintenance, corporate fit (into your business), references, and your assessment of their facility and business. You may also consider interviewing potential new suppliers just as you would do so with potential new employees, i.e. visit their facility(ies), conduct an audit(s) of their systems, and interview and/or speak with their key people as well.

Once you've investigated and scored all your potential suppliers, simply multiply their scores for each criteria times the criteria weighting, add up all their weighted scores, and let your purchasing decision matrix process reveal the best supplier for your particular purchase. You may not like the result of this process—that's okay. If you question your first result, you may consider reviewing your selection criteria, the weighting you've assigned to each item, and each supplier's criteria score. But in the end, you may be just fooling yourself. I advise you allow this purchasing matrix method to remove any personal bias you may have for any particular supplier(s); that's its purpose: to help you make the best supplier selection for your business based on the criteria that you've selected. After deciding which supplier will win the job, I recommend you always first inform the winning supplier and then all the other potential suppliers as soon as you can thereafter. You may be surprised how unsuccessful, potential suppliers may thank you for calling them with the news that they did not win the bid. In the end, they are people too and want to know either way. For those non-winning, potential suppliers who ask, I also recommend you offer constructive feedback that they can use for their next bid(s).

I suggest the above step of contacting and working with non-winning bid suppliers is important for another reason: back up suppliers. Think about this: how will you protect your business and customers against a current supplier bankruptcy, change of ownership, or a natural disaster, preventing them from delivering components and/or services to your company? I propose it is critical for your business, especially if it operates on very short product and/or service delivery lead times, to establish and have ready at least one backup supplier for each critical component and/or service required to deliver your company's product and/or service. You may also consider regularly alternating and/or sharing the awarding of contracts for a common product and/or service among two or three qualified suppliers for this very reason. This strategy of alternate and/or shared sourcing may not be well received by some of your suppliers, but it may be a prudent way to ensure a consistent and stable supply to your business.

Unfortunately, you may need to deal with current or potential suppliers who may offer you and/or your employees a bribe(s) in return for business. In the rare case when a bribe or "favour" has been offered to me personally, I politely declined and then immediately began the process of de-sourcing that current or potential supplier. My advice is you consider firing any employee on the spot if you have evidence they actually accepted any supplier bribe or "favour" in return for business. I recommend that you, as I do, never associate with anyone who does business by offering bribes or favours for personal enrichment such as financial payments, vacations, cars, etc. I further recommend you consider, as I have always done, awarding business to another supplier, even with a slightly higher price, to avoid granting business to a supplier who offered some bribe or "favour" in return for business. In one extraordinary situation (at least to me), I personally de-sourced a current supplier who offered me regular monthly payments to be directly deposited into my bank account in return for "making any quality and/or delivery problem(s) with his product(s) go away." Funny, this same future ex-supplier then told me some time later I was responsible for his employees being laid off as a result of losing their supply contract with our business. As I have said before, my advice is to stay away from any potential or current supplier who offers you and/or anyone in your company any bribe or "favour" resulting in personal enrichment in return for business.

But in the real business world, you may have a current or potential supplier(s) who wants to take you out for lunch or some other event, offers your company a gift as a golf tournament prize, or free t-shirts for your employees. I recommend you establish and clearly communicate your policy about employees accepting gifts to all your potential and current suppliers and employees. I also recommend you include your employee gift policy in your employee handbook and enforce it without exception. Despite saying "no thank you" to all supplier gift offers, I have found a few suppliers who insist leaving me a small gift, especially around Christmas time. In these cases, I always raffle off such gifts to my employees, thus accomplishing three objectives: it allows me to reward my employees, to avoid profiting personally from such gifts, and it shows my employees I follow my own policy.

Now that you have sourced your supplier(s), how do you manage them? Very simply, by implementing a supplier development program. Your supplier development program may include producing and distributing a supplier manual that your suppliers agree constitute part of their contract with your company. Your supplier manual may include your business hours of operation, contact lists, packaging specifications, access instructions to a supplier portal on your company website, and details on how your suppliers can submit cost savings ideas to your company.

You may even volunteer to visit your supplier's facility to conduct a VA/VE (value analysis value engineering) workshop to identify potential costs savings to help them meet your company's cost savings targets. I recall a personal experience where I visited a key supplier's facility and conducted such a week-long VA/VE workshop. At first, their management group was somewhat hesitant to participate, but everyone fully participated in the exercises once they realized I was sincere in my efforts to help them. In fact, during this week, we identified numerous cost savings ideas that resulted in cost savings that far exceeded our company's current year cost savings target. In turn, our supplier kept the remaining cost savings for themselves, which was good for our business as well: a profitable supplier ensured a stable supply for our company, it facilitated supplier cost savings for the following year's targets, and demonstrated that we truly wanted to partner with them.

In addition to your supplier manual and conducting a VA/VE workshop(s), you may also consider developing and implementing a supplier performance tracking methodology to measure your suppliers' quality, on-time delivery, fill rates, and cost savings proposals. You may also include your regular supplier facility audit results (this is when your employees visit your suppliers' facilities to audit their quality and business system procedures) into your supplier performance ratings. Typically, your supplier performance database is maintained by your materials, shipping and receiving, and quality personnel. From these measurables, you can develop a supplier performance scorecard distributed on a regular basis. I also recommend your business acknowledges your top three suppliers on an annual basis by inviting them and some of their employees to your facility for an award, plant tour, and lunch. Although supplier development and recognition programs may seem to require some time and effort at first, I suggest your company will be rewarded multiple times with a stable supply of supplier products and/or services delivered with the expected quality, on-time, and at costs mutually beneficial to both parties.

Some final thoughts on suppliers: as with all critical relationships, I suggest a key value of any customer-supplier relationship is honesty. Although both you and your suppliers need to ensure your businesses are profitable, I suggest mutual honesty and integrity will ensure both parties win in the long run. I suggest you consider, as I always have, the true test of any good supplier is how they react and support your business even when your company is responsible for an issue(s). In such situations, your valued supplier(s) may have the means to help your company, do so without hesitation, and may not even charge your business for doing so. When you find such a supplier, my advice is to stick with them despite most future potential challenges. On the other hand, you may find yourself in a situation where a valued supplier has genuinely lost money on a job, typically caused by some of their own internal issues, but continued to deliver their product and/or service with the required quality, on-time, and at the agreed upon price. On such occasions, you may consider permitting your valued supplier to recoup some of their losses within reason on future jobs as long as they remain relatively competitive. As with all critical relationships in business and life, I propose they require some *give and take* by both parties.

## For More Information and Advice

Please contact us at www.chargeupyourbusinessbook.com and/or www.gbicego.com if you would like more information and advice for your quoting, costing, and pricing challenges such as the importance of quoting, costing and pricing, quoting strategies, costing strategies, pricing strategies, supplier selection and purchasing, and/or any other challenges—we are here to help.

# CHAPTER 3

# YOUR CUSTOMERS

## Customer Focus & Service

Who is your customer? Many people answer this question by identifying the person and/or company that receives the benefits of their product and/or service. The issue with this thinking is sometimes the person and/or company receiving the benefits of your product and/or service may not always directly pay your business in return for those benefits. For example, you may sell your product and/or service to someone who in turn may offer it to someone else as an end user. Who is your customer in this scenario? Business can be thought of as an exchange of value between two parties. In your case, your business may provide a product and/or service in return for something of value, typically in the form of financial payment.

I propose your customer is any person and/or business that actually pays your company and/or has the authority to pay your business in return for your product and/or service. At times, your customer is also your end user, but sometimes your customer is not the end user of your product and/or service. This customer definition does not imply that you and your business should ignore the needs of the end users of your product and/or service. If you do, you may endanger your business altogether since the needs of your end users are connected with the needs of your customers. My advice is that you and your business should always remain focused on meeting your customers' needs, since they directly return value to your business, while simultaneously concentrating on the requirements of your product and/or service end users.

What kind of company are you? What does your business do? When I ask these questions to a group, I typically receive responses such as "we are here to make money and/or grow the business" from management personnel, to replies such as "we are here to get paid," from other employees. Some answers are focused on the design and/or manufacturing of the product(s) or service(s) the business provides. I suggest your business can be considered as a customer delivery enterprise. Let me explain: you can establish your business by investing resources, people, time, money, equipment, building, etc. to design and manufacture a product and/or service. But if your business never ships your product and/or service to any customer and is reimbursed in return, all you will have is a large inventory of unsold product and/or service. As more and more people in your company accept that your business is a delivery enterprise based on your customers' needs, suddenly your shipper becomes the most important position in the company. Your shipper typically is your business's last contact with your customers before your product and/or service is actually delivered. I suggest this philosophy benefits your business because your shipper may at times struggle to receive your business's product and/or service from your production group in order to meet your customers' needs. Below is one of my personal experiences how I implemented this philosophy which demonstrates its resulting benefits.

I assumed responsibility for a business and quickly noticed how little finished product was available every morning for that day's shipments—forget about tomorrow's or the next day's deliveries. In fact, sometimes we upset our customers by missing some customer shipment delivery dates altogether. There was also a *product hot sheet* distributed by our shipper every morning, listing what product items and quantities were required to be shipped that afternoon. Every day, our shipper would run around the plant pleading with production to prepare products for that day's shipments—he would usually be the last person to leave late every night. I was told this situation occurred for years and asked our shipper what he needed. He replied, "Right product, ready at the right time." That's a simple and good answer— our shipper was customer-focused but it seemed the rest of the company was not as customer-focused as he was at the time. When I asked why he doesn't have the "right product at the right time" on a regular basis, our shipper replied, "No one takes shipping and our customers' needs seriously; production makes whatever products they want, when they want."

Immediately, right then and there, and every morning thereafter for a few short weeks, I personally accompanied our shipper when he spoke with production supervisors to remind them what products and quantities he/our customers needed that day and beyond. Very quickly, the production supervisors learned that when the shipper and I came to see them, it was in their own best interest to have the required products or a plan to deliver them to the shipping area that day. Within a few days, the shipper began receiving products and quantities for the current day's customer shipments and for the next few days after that. In fact, our shipper was receiving so many finished goods ahead of time that he needed to arrange floor space to organize it all. Within a few weeks, I began noticing our shipper was leaving work on time at the end of his regular shift and sometimes even early because the day's shipments were already done!

This exercise resulted in several benefits: it re-focused all my employees' activities and priorities to serving our customers' needs, we consistently met all our customer delivery requirements, and we had happy customers. There were additional benefits such as we learned how to quickly changeover our processes to meet customer demands, we reduced our overtime costs, and increased our profits.

What is good customer service? Who does customer service in your business? I advise customer service is not a to-do item; I suggest it is a mindset, a corporate value that must be shared by yourself and every employee (not just your customer service department if you have one) since it is critical to your business success. I propose good customer service occurs when your customers feel their particular need(s) is met within reasonable limits through their relationship with your business. I advise you and your employees must always consider your business's medium to long term objectives when dealing with any customer issue(s). Although resolving a customer issue may seem to have short-term negative consequences for your business, I suggest you consider doing so may provide your business another opportunity to provide your customer even more value at a later time. It is well documented that it may cost your business more money to develop new customers from new sources than obtaining repeat business from your current customers. Think of the times when you have received great customer service from a company. How did you feel afterwards? Would you buy again and refer other customers to this company? Of course. In the end, great customer service just means good business.

I sometimes cringe when I hear statements such as "the customer is number one" or "the customer is always right." Yes, customers are very important to your business because, without them, I propose you have no chance of any revenue to pay yourself, your employees, or any other business costs—or have any money left over for profit. I suggest you consider your customers are not always *number one.* When you are in business, I suggest your business is *number one.* By *your business,* I am referring to the people who actually make up and work in your business, you, and your employees. I suggest this viewpoint because without a fully functioning business, your customer's needs will not be met. I have seen too many examples where business people modify their processes, products, and/or services to satisfy some ridiculous customer requirement(s), only to wipe out their profits and then potentially their business. Sometimes you might consider that it may be more advantageous for your business to fire a bad customer than to lose your good employees and/or your entire business itself.

## Project/Program Management

A customer has awarded an order to your business or you may have decided to proceed with a project internally—you plan to increase revenues and/or reduce costs by purchasing a new piece of equipment. Congratulations! You reviewed the quotes, the equipment salesperson guaranteed everything will work out better than expected, you have high expectations, paid a deposit, and delegated the project to one of your team members to follow-up and keep you updated on a regular basis. Time goes by and you've heard nothing, so you may think "no news is good news." Finally, the project due date arrives when you learn it is behind schedule and mired in all sorts of equipment, supplier, and quality problems, no one knows exactly what's going on, it's now going to cost more, and the equipment will not deliver what was promised to your customer or to your business—in fact, less. Less for more money and more time! What happened? How does this situation occur over and over again, and why? What's the solution? The solution is effective project management.

There are several keys to effective program management such as establishing a well-defined project scope with a set of deliverables, realistic timing and budget expectations, and clear expectations from all parties involved at every project stage/milestone. I recommend you appoint a single project co-ordinator who will be responsible for all program management activities such as quoting, customer specifications, purchasing, suppliers, etc. I also recommend regular project update or status meetings with senior management to obtain resources, overcome any obstacles, and to ensure a successful project implementation. Finally, I suggest you obtain buy-ins and approvals from all parties involved with the project, such as customers, suppliers, and in-house resources such as production, quality, shipping/receiving, maintenance, HR, etc. I expand on some of these keys to effective program management below.

Time. You cannot make any more of it, and it sometimes seems there is never enough of it. After a project scope and set of deliverables have been established and a project coordinator appointed, one of your first program management steps is to develop your project timing. A project timeline is constructed by first identifying and listing all the project tasks in their correct order with their individual duration times. Then you link all the individual tasks related to each other under major subtasks. This is the vast majority of *work* when designing a project timeline which may require hours, days, or sometimes weeks, depending on the project scope and time duration. I recommend you identify the project timeline *critical path* which consists of a series of tasks that must occur in a specific sequence within a specific timeframe that will ultimately determine the overall project completion timing. I also recommend you regularly monitor how any task(s) or series of tasks may affect your *critical path* and thus overall project timing. I also advise that your project coordinator regularly updates their timeline and meets/follows-up with all project parties to ensure their tasks are completed on time or even early.

There are several methods and/or software programs that can be used to document your project timeline. I recommend you consider using the Microsoft Project software to design and maintain project timelines, especially if your project duration is over a month or so. With Microsoft Project, you can list all your tasks, the sequence of tasks, and design that certain tasks need to be completed before others can start. You can also set project milestones and detail your project costs, resource allocations, and usages. I suggest at least one of your employees use MS Project to manage all your major projects.

Money. Similar to time, sometimes it seems there never is enough money. Similar to tracking your project timing with a timeline, I propose it is critical to first budget and then track all your costs as the project progresses to compare your actual costs to your budgeted ones. When budgeting for any project, some people may tend to just focus on obvious costs such as equipment purchases or design fees. I recommend you also include freight, duty, exchange rates, installation, commissioning, maintenance, and other related costs in every project budget. If you are approaching your project budget *magic number* and may require more funds, I suggest you provide your supervisor and/or whomever is financing the project a heads up and have this issue addressed as soon as possible. I also recommend you complete an actual vs. budget cost review once your project is completed. At first you may not want to complete an actual vs. budget cost review, especially if your project costs went over budget. Regardless, I suggest an actual vs. budget cost review is a very useful exercise to confirm how you've performed financially on a project and, most importantly, will provide guidance for any future projects. Although you may track your project costs with Microsoft Project, I recommend you consider using, as I do, Microsoft Excel to develop a project budget and track all your project costs.

Follow-up, follow-up, follow-up. Follow-up is another very important key to successful program management. In fact, I suggest follow-up may be the most important task a successful program manager performs day in and day out. I recommend that a project coordinator must always be following up on every aspect of their project, and how the early or late completion of any task(s) may affect the critical path and/or project budget. Being a project manager may seem at times like monotonous, frustrating work, especially when you are going from meeting to meeting, and from visit to visit, to meeting. But I propose that consistent, effective follow-up must be done to ensure your project is completed early/on time and on (or even better, below) budget. I cannot tell you how many times I have seen projects stall and/or *go bad* very quickly due to lack of follow-up; it's not pretty.

A final key to successful project management is my recommendation to always complete a trial run/ buy-off at the supplier's facility before releasing any equipment for delivery to your facility. You may have experienced when your brand new piece of non-working equipment sits on your production floor while your customer is waiting to sign off a brand new process. Why does this happen? I suggest one major reason may be that there was no effective equipment trial run or buy-off completed at your equipment supplier's facility before delivery. Let me ask you: Would you test drive a car before purchasing it? Do you typically preview or tour a home before renting or buying it? Do you try on a pair of shoes before buying them? Then why would you, or anyone for that matter, ever think of receiving and purchasing a piece of equipment before trying it out at your supplier's facility? I suggest that not completing a trial run at your equipment supplier's facility before delivery may cause additional time delays, costs, frustrations, and perhaps loss of your business credibility in the eyes of your customer(s). I also advise you to consider sending everyone who will be in contact with your new piece of equipment (such as your health and safety, quality, maintenance, production operators) to your supplier's facility to conduct a trial run(s) to ensure you have everyone's approvals/buy-ins before the equipment arrives at your facility—even if you may need to delay its shipment.

## For More Information and Advice

Please contact us at www.chargeupyourbusinessbook.com and/or www.gbicego.com if you would like more information and advice for your customer challenges such as customer service and focus, project management and/or any other challenges—we are here to help.

# PART II – YOUR OPERATIONS

# CHAPTER 4

# SAFETY & THE ENVIRONMENT

## The Importance of Safety

I recommend that the health and safety of your employees must always be your number one operations priority, since it takes care of your greatest business asset: your people. I propose there is nothing more important than your own safety, and the health and safety of your employees and co-workers. Nothing. I suggest everyone should always think safety first before they do anything. Perhaps you may have seen, as have I, too many people with permanent life injuries as a result of a work accident because of carelessness and sometimes negligence. It is your personal and your management's responsibility to design and implement a health and safety program, and to implement its policies fairly and consistently. But it is also all your employees' responsibility to follow those policies and practices at all times, and to report any potential health and safety issues.

I suggest you always speak frankly, as I do, about safety because it is a serious issue. Perhaps one of the reasons I have always been so passionate about people's safety is because I've unfortunately seen how accidents not only affect those people who suffer injuries, but also their families and their co-workers. Trust me, accidents can affect everyone involved and sometimes for the rest of their lives. You may go out in the world every day to earn an income to support yourself, your loved ones, and to contribute to society in whatever way(s) you choose. If you get hurt, it is you who suffers that injury (and that injury may also affect your family and friends) twenty-four hours a day, seven days a week, until you heal (if you heal). If there are longer lasting effects of an injury for the rest of your life, it is you and your family whose income may be affected—and that's a reason you run a business or go to work in the first place. After an injured employee is dropped off at the local clinic or hospital, life typically goes on at the business as usual, but that employee remains injured. It is the harsh reality; that's why I advise you it is never worth taking a risk with your own, and especially others', health and safety.

## Your Safety Program

I recommend your health and safety program be designed and implemented by both management and worker employees to be effective and to at least meet minimum legislative requirements. Every jurisdiction has workplace safety regulations in place that must be met; I suggest you always strive to exceed them whenever feasible. I suggest another critical *ingredient* of your effective health and safety program is genuine support from you and your senior business leadership to champion initiatives and remove any bureaucratic or other obstacles. I say *genuine* senior business leadership support because too many times I have witnessed, and perhaps you may have, senior leadership people say they support their health and safety program but then do not do much more than pay *lip service* to its initiatives or, worse, do something(s) that contradicts health and safety policies and practices. For example, not wearing personal protective equipment (PPE) while in the presence of other employees who may or may not be doing the same. I offer you one secret to permanently implementing an effective health and safety program: have yourself and all your senior management personnel follow every health and safety program requirement and guideline at all times without exceptions, i.e. lead by *do what I do* versus *do what I say, not what I do*. I suggest when everyone else sees you and all the bosses wearing their PPE, it will provide the rest of the management team incredibly more leverage to ensure everyone else always wears their

PPE. And if anyone sees you, one of the *bosses*, or any other visitor not wearing their PPE, I suggest you encourage your employees to politely remind them to wear their PPE immediately before proceeding.

I recommend to start your effective health and safety program activities with your annual health and safety strategic plan separate from any other business planning document or exercise. I suggest your annual health and safety strategic plan should be based upon and review any past accident, incident, and potential hazards data and then suggest goals and strategies to improve the health and safety of all your employees. Don't have any meaningful or detailed accident/ incident/potential hazards data from the past year? Then I strongly recommend you confirm them before proceeding with your plan. I also recommend your annual health and safety strategic plan contain your annual health and safety budget and training program that should also be separate items in your overall business budget.

I propose a very important aspect of your health and safety program is an effective Joint Health & Safety Committee (JHSC), or at least a safety representative(s), depending on the number of employees in your company. Typically, management picks/asks/or *volunteers* both management and worker employee JHSC members. I advise you consider using this opportunity to have both management and worker employee JHSC members elected by all employees (and not by management). Your business will benefit from the election of JHSC members as follows: it gives all employees a sense of contribution that they can affect what happens in the workplace (and that is very good), and it dramatically raises the JHSC's credibility. Typically, JHSC members' elections are held every year. At first, your employees may not be familiar with, or may be skeptical about, this concept to elect their own JHSC members, so senior management may need to ask some employees the first time to get the process going. I also recommend every JHSC meeting minutes should be taken, distributed, and reviewed as the first order of business at the following JHSC meeting. Depending on your business jurisdiction, it may be necessary to train some JHSC members as certified members. I also suggest you train at least one JHSC member on how to effectively facilitate the JHSC (or any) meetings.

I recommend another key aspect of your effective health and safety program is regular workplace inspections completed by the JHSC. I recommend at least monthly JHSC workplace inspections, that all findings or hazards be recorded, categorized as "A" (most urgent), "B", or "C", and responsibilities and target dates assigned for each identified hazard. I also advise that you, or a senior management person, participate in workplace inspections, and your and their involvement must be sincere. This practice has the following benefits: it may offer the management person more insights into the business, and it demonstrates to all employees your and management's genuine commitment to safety. I also suggest you post and distribute all your workplace inspections as required. In addition to regular workplace inspections, I recommend a potential hazards reporting program is another effective way to allow employees to identify and report potentially dangerous conditions that, if left unchecked, may lead to an accident(s).

Accident investigations are also a part of your effective health and safety program. Of course, accident investigations are normally reactionary in nature and your goal is to minimize any accidents from occurring in the first place. But I suggest it is critical that a proper accident investigation be conducted after the injured employee is cared for. In some jurisdictions, there may be minimum reporting time frames from which an accident must be reported to the appropriate government agency. A properly completed accident investigation can become an effective part of your health and safety program presenting opportunities for improvement. I recommend you take advantage of this (hopefully very rare) occasion to improve the health and safety of all your employees.

Depending on your business operations, an occupational illness program may be required as a component of your overall health and safety program. Occupational illnesses may include air quality, noise levels and hearing tests, and designated hazardous substances—I suggest you check your local jurisdiction regulations. For example, you may need or should conduct annual noise surveys and then implement strategies to reduce any noise hazards for your employees. There are many effective and low cost ways to accomplish this. You may consider conducting annual hearing tests for your employees, but a word of caution: in my experience, annual hearing tests may become a *double edged sword*. On one hand, you are being proactive and documenting any hearing loss that may or may not be caused by your work environment over several years. For example, I have been told by hearing test providers that hearing test results may be affected by the person's health (e.g. if a person has a cold or is taking prescription medication(s)). On the other hand, hearing tests may also unnecessarily heighten awareness, leading some employees to become needlessly concerned about their natural hearing loss with age, unless they are exposed to constant high levels of noise on a regular basis. Another example of an occupational illness program is associated with a business I once ran containing a lead die casting process. To ensure the health and safety of our employees and meet relevant industrial regulations, we regularly sent our lead die-casting employees for annual blood and urine tests. Thankfully, those employees had blood and urine lead levels far below maximum limits as stated within local health regulations.

I recommend a first aid program must be part of your health and safety program and business operations. At minimum, I suggest you have at least one person trained as a certified first-aider for each department and/or each shift. I also suggest you post pictures and certificates of all your first-aiders, and that their training be reviewed and maintained at least on an annual basis. I also advise your company to set up a first aid room(s), complete with an eye wash station (perhaps also have eye wash stations strategically located throughout your facility), a sink, stretcher(s), master first aid supply cabinet, list of emergency contact telephone numbers (both management and outside emergency services), and lists, maps, and directions to the nearest walk-in clinic(s) and hospital(s). I suggest first aid kits be strategically located throughout your facility, maps be posted on bulletin boards showing their locations, and large clear signs be used denoting their locations. I also suggest the contents of all first aid kits and the master first aid supply cabinet be part of all regular workplace inspections. A standard list of contents for each first aid kit should be checked regularly, and supplies should be replenished as required. Even if not required by law, you may also consider having and training all your employees to use an automated external defibrillator (AED) located at your facility.

I advise an emergency preparedness program must be another part of your health and safety program and should be reviewed at least annually. Your emergency preparedness plan may include instructions, procedures, maps, and directions to be followed in case of required evacuations. I suggest you consider implementing a minimum number of *practice* evacuations every year, but never announce them. You may also track your progress on how well your employees evacuate your building(s) over time and implement any procedural improvements. Your emergency preparedness plan should also describe how your business may deal with both natural and human-made disasters such as tornadoes, hurricanes, extreme weather storms, and medical emergencies such as large scale social health infections, electrical power and water supply failures, and bomb threats. Your emergency preparedness plan may also list critical suppliers and how your business will recover if any one of them may no longer be able to supply your business, thus threatening your product and/or service supply to your customers.

Finally, I recommend an extensive training program be another crucial part of your effective health and safety program. I suggest your health and safety training plan be reviewed at least annually and take into consideration any past accidents, reported hazards, and any new training required by legislation. I advise your health and safety training program include less frequent training such as JHSC member certification, management/supervisor/employee safety requirements under the law, or accident investigations trainings. I also advise you consider regular employee health and safety trainings such as annual chemical hazards training, forklift or crane training, emergency preparedness and practice evacuation drills, or any other training(s) that may be required to keep all your employees healthy and safe throughout the year.

## Accidents & Claims Management

An accident has happened. Your injured employee will fully recover—hopefully. The immediate crisis may be over and it's "back to business as usual." Not so fast. I suggest when any employee becomes injured at work, regardless if it is a physical or mental injury, that injury may affect everyone in your organization, even if you lead a multi-national organization. I suggest it is very important that you take care of your remaining employees after an injured employee is in treatment. You may consider hiring a social worker in some cases to help your remaining employees deal with any after effects of a severe accident, especially for those who may have witnessed the accident and/or tried to help your critically injured employee. I advise you keep anyone who inquires updated with the latest news regarding the injured employee's progress without divulging any personal or confidential information. I also recommend you keep all your employees informed on a regular basis of what is being done to prevent any recurrences of any accident. In my opinion, regular updates will go a long way to assure everyone that you are on top of the situation and they continue to work in a safe environment.

I also recommend your company design and implement a return-to-work program whenever an injured employee is capable of resuming work. Even if your injured employee can only perform modified work at first, I still recommend you bring them to part-time or full-time employment as soon as possible. This strategy has at least two benefits: first and foremost it helps your injured employee recover holistically and quicker to reintegrate into your company, and secondly will help minimize any employee health and safety premiums that may be incurred by your business. To facilitate your injured employee's return, I recommend you contact and work with them, their health professional(s), and any other government agency as soon as feasible. You may also consider designing an individual, formal return-to-work program and timeline specific to your injured employee's needs with the aid of any related job function analyses.

## Work Refusals & Stoppages

Work refusals and stoppages may sometimes occur in your company and are an integral part of your health and safety program. I suggest a difference between a work refusal and work stoppage is that a work refusal typically occurs before the work is started, and a work stoppage typically occurs while the work is in progress. In my experiences, work refusals and stoppages occur when there is a legitimate employee concern about a task that they've been asked to complete, or a process that has been already initiated. But I also suggest that, in some cases, some individuals may want to *pull out the safety card* just to avoid completing a task assigned to them or allowing the process to continue just to cause trouble for whatever reason(s). Here is how I always personally handle and advise you to deal with any work refusal or stoppage. Simply ask two questions: "Is there a safety issue?" and "Is there a training issue?"  If your concerned employee replies yes to either question(s), I strongly recommend that you isolate any danger(s) and rectify any legitimate issue(s) immediately. If there is a legitimate training issue, I suggest you train the concerned individual immediately, if feasible, or have another properly trained employee complete the task while addressing the training needs of your currently *untrained* employee.

If your "concerned" employee truthfully answers *no* to both questions, or *yes* but you suspect or know they may be deceitful, I suggest you consider to quickly and firmly show the "concerned" individual that you will not support or accept their refusal to complete the task. This is where your judgment and diplomacy skills come in handy. I suggest that if you speak prudently, your "concerned" employee may admit there may not be a genuine safety and/or training issue. If your "concerned" employee persists in their work refusal or stoppage, I advise you consider suggesting that their continuing behaviour may be considered as insubordination. Hopefully, once your "concerned" employee understands where they stand on this issue, they may complete the task assigned, assuming there is no safety or training issue. As a last resort, you may consider contacting an appropriate outside party to resolve any work stoppage or refusal dispute.

Despite any potential artificial employee safety "concerns," I strongly recommend you (as I always have personally) support the right of any employee to refuse or stop any work, and report any legitimate potential health and safety concern(s) to their appropriate supervisor(s). I also strongly advise you to support an employee's action to contact the local labour ministry as a last resort after they have legitimately exhausted all internal company channels. I also advise you, as I have, discipline and reprimand any manager and supervisor who ignores any employees' health and safety concern(s). I recommend to always first consider any employee's work refusal or stoppage as legitimate, and ask two questions: "Is there a safety issue?" and "Is there a training issue?" and then proceed accordingly.

## Your Environment Program

I suggest that environment program and initiatives must be part of your overall health and safety program. In some large organizations, environment may be a total separate department with its own director, budget, annual strategic plan, and initiatives. I recommend you achieve your business environmental goals in whatever manner and format that makes sense for your business. I propose that many ideas and strategies discussed in the previous health and safety section (such as an environmental strategic plan, budget, training, inspections, and emergency preparedness) can be used to develop your environment program, so I will not repeat them here. Instead, in this section, I offer you my best advice when implementing an effective environment program and how to deal with any potential environment issue(s) associated with your business.

I recommend one of the best things you can do for your business from an environment point of view is to hire a professional environment consultant to conduct a facility environmental audit. I also recommend that your environment consultant have detailed knowledge about the regulations within your business jurisdiction, a relevant background and experience in dealing with appropriate government agencies. I suggest it is crucial that you hire an environmental consultant who ideally has a chemistry, biochemistry, and/or engineering background—in some cases, you may even consider retaining a qualified environment lawyer. Your business environmental issues have a potential to cause great harm to the environment in general, your employees, and business operations, including substantial costs and fines in some cases. To avoid potential dangers to the environment, and to your employees' health and business operations, I strongly recommend you always *do the right thing* when dealing with environment and other issues such as safety, quality, etc.

The purpose of conducting a facility environment audit is to provide you a baseline or starting point for your environment initiatives and may result in creating additional environment program objectives. An audit demonstrates your commitment and due diligence to your employees and any interested government agency, and may also unexpectedly uncover some previously unknown dire situation(s). You may then be in a position to revise your environment strategic plan and initiatives to address any imminent, medium, or long term environmental issues, depending on the results of your environment facility audit. For example, you may find a leaking underground tank that requires to be emptied to prevent further damage to the environment and any nearby underground water table. Another audit result may be the discovery that your building contains some old asbestos insulation or polychlorinated biphenyls (PCBs) in your transformers. At this point, I strongly advise you take immediate action(s) to mitigate any dangers to your employees and the environment.

Government environment protection agencies have a purpose to prevent potential environmental disasters and enforce environmental laws in your business jurisdiction. In fact, government environment agency officers may have the authority to shut down your entire facility and its operations without your consent based solely on their findings; this power may be rarely used but very effective at times, allowing them to enforce environmental laws and regulations. I recommend that you, as I do, respect and work with any government agency person who visits your business. You may find environment government agency people to be fair and just want to help you and your business remain within the applicable environmental laws. I advise you complete any environmental order task(s) quickly, and submit any results and order completion confirmation ahead of schedule if possible. I also advise you notify the appropriate environmental agency person(s) if your business may be delayed to implement an environmental order. I also recommend you consider implementing suggestions made during an environment government agency visit(s) that may not have been included in any official order(s), and to send confirmation(s) that these suggestions were also implemented.

## For More Information and Advice

Please contact us at www.chargeupyourbusinessbook.com and/or www.gbicego.com if you would like more information and advice for

your safety challenges such as the importance of safety, your safety program, accident and claims management, work refusals and stoppages, your environment program and/or any other challenges— we are here to help.

# CHAPTER 5

# QUALITY

## The Importance of Quality

Many people think and acknowledge the latest *modern quality revolution* was led by Japanese manufacturers after World War II. You may recall some Japanese companies were not always recognized for their product quality. Eventually, these same Japanese manufacturers became known for their superior product quality after implementing and improving ideas introduced to them by Dr. Deming. It may have seemed the rest of the world had to play *catch up* to duplicate improved Japanese product quality since then and even today; many Japanese products enjoy a very good reputation for high quality.

I recommend the quality of your product(s) and/or service(s) should always be your number two operations priority, after your number one operations priority of employee health and safety, because it takes care of your customers. Without customers, your business simply will not receive any income to pay for your expenses and generate profits. I propose your product and/or service quality is crucial to your business's success, and its importance must be driven by you *from the top*, similar to employee safety. It is disappointing that some companies hire quality assurance people and create and implement quality systems and procedures, only to have the importance of these initiatives diminished by a senior leader's decision(s) and/or actions. I suggest it may only require one decision or action by you and/or a senior business leader to destroy the concept of good quality as an important business value.

I propose good quality is critical to your business's success, especially in an ever increasingly competitive marketplace. You and your business may be excused for one quality "spill," especially if your company acknowledges and deals with it quickly and effectively. But any continued quality "spills" may be dealt with ruthlessly by the marketplace consisting of your customers. Here's a story I usually tell to demonstrate and emphasize the importance of quality.

Suppose you purchase fruit from a local supermarket—you check it, seems fine, put it into your cart, pay for it, and bring it home. A day or so later, you find the fruit has gone bad beyond any reasonable expectations. So, you return the bad fruit where the store management provides you replacement fruit at no charge, with an apology, if they value you as a customer. The store management may also follow-up with you as to why you previously received bad fruit, and explains what they will do to prevent any recurrence. The store in this case wisely corrected a *mistake* of providing some bad fruit but quickly and effectively addressed your issue. In most cases, you as the customer will return to the same supermarket, and you may tell others how well you were received and how your problem was resolved. All these actions will result to maintain and increase the store's number of paying customers.

On the other hand, some stores may argue with you as a customer returning bad fruit beyond reasonable expectations and may refuse to provide you with any new replacement fruit. At this point, you as the customer can either continue shopping at this store (due to other reasons such as low cost and/or location) or take your business to another store. The supermarket had one chance to rectify your customer issue and failed to address it. Now, you as a customer may return to that same supermarket and take another chance to purchase additional fruit and/or other items. And if you purchased another defective piece of fruit, or any other defective item, the chances that you may leave that store forever as a customer increases with every incident whenever your quality expectations were not met.

I suggest every time your business does not meet any customer's quality expectations, you increase the probability of losing not only that customer but everyone else they communicate with who are current and/or could have been potential new customers. Your dissatisfied ex-customer(s) may even blog about their bad experience and poorly rate your business. As a result, your business may unnecessarily suffer, even if you feel their comments are inaccurate. I suggest some of your current and future potential customers may shop elsewhere and pay a higher price for a better quality product and/or service if your business does not quickly and effectively correct every quality incident(s). In today's competitive world, your business may only have one or perhaps very few (if you're lucky) chance(s) to correct any customer quality incident before your customer (and everyone they communicate with) moves their business and your business revenue elsewhere—sometimes forever.

## Who is Responsible for Quality?

A popular quality philosophy is that "quality is everyone's responsibility." This quote is attributed to Dr. Deming, and I agree this statement is generally correct. Typically, in many, and perhaps in your company, there may be a quality assurance function which in my opinion is required in all organizations in one form or another.

You may have employees who rely on your quality personnel to check their work and verify your product or service quality before it is delivered to your end customers. Unfortunately, on occasion, you may also hear statements such as "I make the product; it's someone else's job to check it" or "quality is someone else's job." These statements and their associated practices are very dangerous for your business and are a symptom that something is very wrong. This philosophy that it is someone else's responsibility to guarantee quality cannot be further from the truth and reality in my opinion. I recommend you primarily hold responsible any process which, and/or person(s) who, contributed to the manufacturing and delivery of any substandard quality product and/or service. I also advise you to hold your quality assurance department accountable to a lesser degree since your quality system did not detect and prevent the substandard quality product and/or service from being manufactured and delivered to your customer(s). Some employees may challenge this viewpoint at which time I suggest you reply by asking, "What or who made the defect?" The answer(s) to this question, such as machine X and/or person Y, will provide a starting point for your investigations and clues for an effective solution(s). When seeking root causes and generating an action plan(s) to address any quality spill, I always recommend you first focus attention on your business process(es) and all its related inputs and outputs, rather than people. This approach will identify the legitimate potential root causes(s) contributing to your quality spill and may eliminate any *blame games* typically associated with such investigations. You may then investigate and address any people issues after exhausting all your potential process root causes. Even then, I recommend you ensure your employee(s) is/are properly trained before focusing on any personnel issue(s).

I assume one of your business operations priorities is your end customers' quality expectations, who are typically located outside your organization. It makes good business sense that you focus on end customer quality expectations since your end customers normally return value/revenue back to your business in exchange for your product(s) and/or service(s). Question: what and/or who determines your end customer's quality? I suggest you consider this answer and viewpoint: the last process step and/or person that touched your product and/or service before reaching the end customer. You may extend this logical thinking until you realize that your entire product and/or service delivery process can be considered a series of process steps and/or people who deliver quality to the next step or person in the sequence. In essence, I propose your business has both external and internal customers. Each operations process step and/or person is the internal customer of the previous process step and/or person. Therefore, I suggest your finished product and/or service quality is determined by the sum of the quality of all your internal business processes/steps and people.

Consider this point: if your product and/or service inherits a defect in step one of ten in your business process, it may hopefully be detected and repaired, if possible, before it causes any issue(s) for step two of ten. But if any defect remains undetected in any step of ten (or, even worse, a defect is detected but nothing is done to resolve that issue), then that defect will almost always (by Murphy's Law) be found by an end customer(s). There's a saying that is applicable when considering your product and/or service quality: "a chain is as strong as the weakest link." Therefore, I suggest you can improve your overall product and/or service quality by focusing on and effectively addressing your business process's *weakest link(s).* In the end, your external customers' expectations are the sum of every internal customers' expectations at every step of your product and/or service delivery process.

## "Too Much" Quality

Before you make any immediate conclusions and respond to these words, let me explain this concept. Meeting your customers' quality expectations is essential to be competitive in any business. Your product and/or service quality level and features are ultimately determined by your marketplace, and you and your business need to decide if you can at least meet or exceed those expectations while meeting your business goals. I suggest that exceeding your customers' quality expectations may be advantageous as long as you can justify doing so by maintaining or growing your market share, increasing revenues, or covering your costs associated with delivering that higher quality and/or features. I suggest this is where your business marketing and branding can be used to convince your customers to pay a higher price and/or wait for your product or service to be manufactured and delivered to them. Consider the success of some high-end quality brands whose product(s) and/or service(s) may seem expensive, and their customers wait months for their delivery, but their quality far exceeds that of their competitors providing a similar product and/or service.

On occasion though, you may encounter a situation where your business provides a product and/or service whose quality far exceeds your customers' expectations and provides no additional value that is justifiable and/or sustainable; in fact, it may unnecessarily cost your business. Believe it or not, and please do not misunderstand me, I suggest there can be at times "too much quality." By now, you may appreciate how much value I personally and also advise you should place on good and even great quality. At the same time, I recommend you consider not making a mistake (in my opinion) to provide your product and/or service with extreme tolerances and/or features that do not add value to or are recognized by to your customers. Committing a *too much quality* mistake without receiving something(s) of value in return for your business may unnecessarily increase your costs such as excess scrap, overtime, and reduced margins. Let me explain using a personal example.

I was appointed program manager for an important project to manufacture and deliver a component integral to the safety system of a larger end product—it was a small but critical part. We proceeded to manufacture prototypes that easily passed all required external and internal functional tests. After we completed a larger quantity product run for initial customer assembly trials, a concern was raised by one of their engineers that my product did not always meet one dimensional tolerance. We immediately investigated this concern and quickly concluded we could not consistently meet this unnecessarily tight tolerance when producing this product in higher volumes without affecting its overall performance (quality). I visited the customer's facility, found where our component was assembled to their larger end product, and promptly concluded this occasionally "out-of-tolerance" dimension had no effect whatsoever on their process. In fact, the manner in which this dimension was sometimes "out of tolerance" actually facilitated an easier assembly process. With this information, I insisted we could not consistently meet this unnecessarily tight dimension tolerance without risking the part function (quality). Eventually, the customer's senior chief engineer visited our facility where I demonstrated our dilemma with production trials, where we created functional parts whose strength met and exceeded their functional requirements but may not have always met this one unreasonable dimension tolerance. We also produced components that consistently met this one insignificant dimension tolerance but may not have met their part functional requirements. I further explained how the manner in which this one dimension is "out of tolerance" at times actually facilitated their assembly process, and this component was never seen by their end customer anyway. In conclusion, I suggested we always maintain and prioritize their functional and strength requirements, and trying to simultaneously maintain this one unreasonable and insignificant dimension tolerance would unnecessarily drive up our costs and their price. Considering these facts, the customer chief engineer quickly agreed with my point of view, granted us a print modification with a larger dimension tolerance for production release, and thanked me for raising and resolving this issue.

Again, please do not misunderstand my point. Great product and/or service quality is essential to your business success. But I also propose you consider not providing your product and/or service with non-value added tolerances and/or features that may not return anything of value to your business and unnecessarily drive up your business costs. I was told once, similar to any destructive addiction, it may be difficult but not impossible to reduce/eliminate your customers' *unnecessarily too high, non-value added* quality habit. It may require some time, lots of negotiations and conversations, and some pain to wean off a customer from their too high, non-value added quality habit that your business inadvertently created in the first place and is now costing too much money. I suggest you try every potential solution to resolve this issue. As a last resort, my advice is that you may need to consider firing your customer(s) if they remain adamant that you maintain your *too high non-value added* quality while your business absorbs what you consider unnecessarily high and unsustainable costs to do so. If you are considering to terminate such a business relationship, I suggest you do so fairly and reasonably while meeting all your obligations to minimize any effects on both your businesses. Personally, I would rather save and preserve my business and employees' jobs to serve other customers versus continuously losing money and/or going bankrupt to serve a customer(s) with an unjustifiable *too high non-value added* quality habit.

## Quality Awareness

Raising your employee quality awareness is a critical strategy to ensuring your product and/or service meets or exceeds your customers' expectations. As with many business priorities, I suggest the value and importance of quality must first come from you, *from the top*. You may find, though, some employees may not appreciate how important quality truly is and how its absence may affect your customers, the business, and their jobs—this is understandable at times. How can you address this challenge?

One strategy to raise employee quality awareness is to bring some employees to, and/or take a video at, your customer's facilities, showing how they use your product and/or service in their business process(es). This visit/video strategy provides your employees with a personal and tangible view as to how your product and/or service is used by your business's customers and re-emphasizes the importance of any particular product feature in your customers' process(es). A customer product and/or process video also demonstrates there is truly another person(s) that uses your business/their product and/or service after it's shipped from your facility. I have completed this exercise a few times with great success.

Another strategy to raise employee quality awareness is to constantly measure your quality performance and present that information to your employees. I suggest most people and employees want to do their job well, fix any issues that may affect quality, and be congratulated and rewarded when they have completed a good job. I have used and seen many positive initiatives, methods, techniques, and strategies to positively promote long-term quality awareness and witnessed many on-going and positive outcomes. But I've also seen some very negative ways to try to promote quality awareness; the worst case I will describe through a personal story below.

I visited a supplier with my quality manager to investigate why their component was causing issues with our product assembly process. During our tour of their plant, I reviewed a list of employee names posted in a display case. It was explained to me that each employee's personal parts rejection rate was calculated and averaged over a time period, and then this worst employee rejection rate list was updated and posted soon after. I could not believe what I was seeing! In the first place, this philosophy assumed that each equipment operator was totally responsible for their equipment process that they could not always control – an invalid assumption in this case. Secondly, I suggest this strategy had little or no chance to positively reinforce anyone's quality commitment over the long term. On the contrary, I noticed coincidently that a small hand-made hammer was placed near the display case obviously expressing employees' disgust and feeling they were being "hammered" by this technique to try to raise employee quality awareness. I propose that any technique based on negative motivation such as shaming an employee's workmanship will not raise overall employee quality awareness in the long term.

Sometimes you may conclude it is not your direct-line employees who may not care about quality, but rather your managers and/or supervisors who do not share your quality values. It is a sad and disturbing situation when your direct-line employees understand and care more about your business product and/or service quality than your manager(s) and supervisor(s) whose job is to support, teach, and guide other employees. But as with every unique situation, there are also unique and effective solution(s). Let me demonstrate using another personal experience.

I was hired to lead a business in which I soon discovered our processes produced excessive defective items that were typically scrapped. It seemed everyone had a reason(s) justifying our current quality and resulting scrap levels. I also confirmed that some supervisors instructed their employees to "keep production going" regardless of the resulting quality level(s). Of course, none of my production supervisors admitted they practiced this *keep production going regardless of quality* policy. My solution: in addition to launching other quality improvement initiatives, I immediately implemented a new policy that all process/product rejects were to be dispositioned during the upcoming weekend only by the production supervisors on whose shift those defects were produced. Guess what happened? The number of defects produced decreased quickly and significantly as the production supervisors themselves began shutting down the manufacturing processes to have our maintenance personnel repair and permanently fix equipment issues that contributed to product defects and scrap. After a short time of absorbing lower throughput and increased overtime costs to supplement lost production while we improved our equipment, we permanently reduced and/or eliminated our product reject and scrap rates, manufacturing costs, and customer quality complaints.

It is a never-ending mission to promote and support the highest possible quality standards for your business product and/or service. At times, it may seem challenging to constantly keep quality (and safety and other priorities) in all your employees' minds. You may make some mistakes while trying to continuously and simultaneously keep quality and safety awareness in your employees' thoughts—that's okay in my opinion. I propose that ensuring your customers receive a high quality product and/or service on-time and at a cost they can afford is the best strategy to maximum your business's success and everyone's job security.

## Supplier Quality

Thus far I have discussed the importance of quality from your external customer's standpoint and within your business through the concepts of internal customers and strategies to raise your employee quality awareness. But I suggest there are other important *players* contributing to your overall business quality performance: your suppliers. Please permit me to expand upon and complete a previous statement: I propose your overall finished product and/or service quality is determined by the sum of the quality of all your internal business processes/steps and employees, and the sum of the quality of all your suppliers' internal business process/steps and their employees. Therefore, I suggest supplier quality is another critical link in your overall business *quality chain.*

I recommend you revisit the end of Chapter 2 to review how to work with and improve your supplier performance and quality.

## For More Information and Advice

Please contact us at www.chargeupyourbusinessbook.com and/or www.gbicego.com if you would like more information and advice for your quality challenges such as the importance of quality, who is responsible for quality, *too much* quality, quality awareness, supplier quality and/or any other challenges—we are here to help.

# CHAPTER 6

# BUSINESS SYSTEMS & CERTIFICATIONS

## The Importance of Business Systems & Certifications

You may be considering that your business will benefit from becoming registered and meeting the requirements of a recognized business certification system. Perhaps one of your customers has made a business system certification a requirement for your company to become a potential new vendor or remain as a current vendor to their business. I suggest some internationally recognized business system certifications were established in an effort to ensure, at least in theory, that registered businesses meet certain design, process, quality, product, and/or other service requirements. I suggest "in theory" because you may be aware that some registered and certified companies have delivered shockingly bad quality products and/or services. You may also find it surprising that some other companies, who are recognized to provide some of the best or very high quality products and/or services, are not certified to, or meet, some internationally recognized business systems standards.

My advice is to consider all the benefits and costs associated with pursuing an *external* internationally recognized business systems certification(s). I also recommend you consider that you may need to turn your current day-to-day business operations upside down to meet an external business system certification(s). Perhaps, having your company become certified to an internationally recognized business certification is just what your business needs at this time to improve its performance. On the other hand, you may consider resisting the temptation to certify your company to an internationally recognized business certification as long as possible until your market place actually demands it. In the end, I recommend you pursue whatever strategy supports your business's objectives and success.

## Steps to Business System Certification

So you have decided that having your business become compliant with an internationally recognized business system certification will improve your company, its operations, and your product and/or service quality. This conclusion is valid as long as you implement practices and procedures that are in compliance with the business standard(s) and it makes sense for your business operations. I advise the last thing you want to do for your business is obstruct any productivity and flexibility by implementing a business system. I suggest it is necessary to find the right balance between your business productivity/flexibility and meeting a business system certification requirements.

After deciding to become compliant with a business system, your first step will be to appoint an internal project coordinator whose first task should be to design a project budget and timeline. I suggest your project coordinator may need to dedicate most or all of their time and efforts at first to achieve your company's business system certification. I also suggest you may need to allocate some of your internal project coordinator's time and efforts, after your company's initial registration, to maintain compliance to your business system. You may also find it beneficial, especially if this is your company's first business system certification, to hire a consultant to guide your project coordinator and business throughout your certification process.

Your second step is to seek out and hire a recognized registrar to help implement your business system. You may be tempted to select a registrar whose costs seem inexpensive and let's say are "lax" and/or "liberal" with their interpretation(s) of a particular certification standard(s). But also be aware that registrars are also audited by their relevant committee/standards people themselves. Therefore, I recommend you select a registrar who has a solid reputation in your marketplace.

Your third step is to have your project coordinator and/or consultant conduct a *gap analysis* to determine how your current business system procedures and practices (if any) compare to the certification standard requirements. Sometimes your consultant is also a recognized business system registrar which may be convenient to both parties. This gap analysis is typically followed by a report and action plan to meet all relevant business system certification prerequisites.

Your fourth, and perhaps most crucial, step is to ensure your procedures and practices meet the desired business system certification standards. I recommend your project coordinator assign tasks for each standard *section* to the appropriate people and/or departments within your organization. I also suggest your project coordinator regularly conduct update or status meetings to ensure everyone stays on track time-wise. It may seem like a lot of work, especially if you and your team are just starting out, but well worth the time and collective efforts to implement procedures and practices to prepare your business to meet your business system certification requirements. I also suggest your project coordinator setup and monitor regular internal audits for your business system practices and procedures. You may also find it valuable to send some of your employees to internal auditor training courses.

Your fifth, and perhaps most nerve-wracking, step is to contact your registrar, set an audit date, proceed with a registration audit, and then get registered—right? Not so fast. It has been my experience that most registrars require anywhere from three to six months of evidence that your company has actually complied with all requirements of a business certification system. I recommend that you include this *evidence collection* phase in your business certification project timeline. After collecting sufficient evidence that your organization meets all business certification requirements, I then recommend that you contact your registrar to complete your registration audit—good luck!

Depending on your business system registration audit results, your sixth step may be to correct any major and/or minor non-conformances found during this appraisal; some registrars may also issue *observances* as suggestions for improvement. Your team may need to implement a corrective action plan(s) as soon as possible after which your registrar will need to confirm those corrective actions are in place before recommending your business for certification. When, or if, no major and/or minor non-conformances exist, congratulations; your business will be recommended for certification! I also recommend you celebrate with all your employees for achieving this milestone!

Now that your business is certified to, and registered with, a particular business certification standard, you may think your work is done. Not so fast again! I strongly recommend at this point that you ensure everyone actually continues to follow all those procedures, process flows, and forms to meet business system requirements. In addition, your business standard certification may require follow-up or minor audits every six months (that may just focus on some areas) and a recertification or major audit (of all areas) every twelve months from your initial registration. I recommend you include these minor and major audits, their costs, and durations when developing your overall project timeline and budget to implement and maintain a fully functioning and certified business system. As you can see, registering for, and becoming certified to, a business standard becomes a *way of doing business* that requires constant focus, discipline, and some resources. I suggest you will most likely conclude that your investment of company efforts and expenditures may result in a more productive and efficient business while improving your customer product and/or service quality.

## Minimum Procedures – Quality

Even if you decide that registering and certifying your organization to a recognized business system standard is not in your company's best interests at the moment, I advise that you document, follow, and enforce as many standard quality and other procedures and practices as feasible. For example, I recommend you implement a few minimum or basic quality ("bad" parts and/or service) identification and corrective actions procedures as follows.

I propose that any final product, sub-component, or any service that does not meet any internal or external customer requirement(s) must be identified and segregated for further processing. The reason for this "bad" product or service identification and segregation is simple: it reduces your probability of delivering a sub-standard end product or service to your customers. "Bad" product and/or service identification can take the form of physically attaching a defect tag on the part, noting the time and date when the defect was discovered and/or produced. It is a good idea, and recommended, that you add a serial number to each defect tag and produce them in duplicate or triplicate, which will facilitate your employees' abilities to track your quality issues with the goal to resolve them as quickly as possible. Your internal defect tagging and inventory procedures also provide an early warning sign of any potential future quality issues that may be experienced by your external paying customers.

I recommend that another minimum quality procedure is to document the resolution of any "bad" part or service after it has been identified—hopefully internally—within your business or by an external customer. There are many procedures and related forms that have been devised to record the resolution of quality issues such as a non-conformance report (NCR), corrective action report (CAR), or an eight-discipline (8D) report. I advise that you always have the responsible department head/ supervisor and their employees involved who actually manufactured and/or delivered the defective product or service actually complete the NCR/CAR/8D report. I suggest this policy will emphasize the importance of quality, hold the appropriate people responsible, and will also have the effect of adding the consequence of additional work associated with any defect produced. If anyone complains about completing such reports, I suggest you reply by stating it is their responsibility to do everything possible to report and avoid producing defects in the first place. I would also remind your employees that this "extra work" is a very small price to pay, especially if the defective product or service was detected internally within your business process(es).

## Some Final Thoughts on Business Systems

Some businesses such as yours, depending on their size and volumes of procedures and documents, may require the services of a part-time or full-time business systems coordinator. I recommend you do not exclude this cost when developing your business system certification budget. Your business systems coordinator does not need to cost you very much, but a very good coordinator's salary and benefits may be returned many times over with improved quality, lower operations costs, and perhaps new business. Typically your business systems coordinator should be detail-oriented, organized, and may be well worth the money to keep your business system(s) certified for decades.

You may have also considered purchasing and implementing a software program that generates all sorts of forms to meet the requirements of a particular business certification standard. Personally, I have never purchased such software and prefer to do everything in-house without a software program—and I recommend you consider doing the same. I suggest following this *do it yourself* strategy will assure increased flexibility to develop your procedures and forms, and your employees will remain better engaged in your business certification process, thus creating a pride of ownership. I suggest you may also find that doing everything in-house is less expensive since you avoid paying your software developer an initial software purchase price, regular license, or update fees, and perhaps any fees to modify their general software program to meet your specific business needs.

I recommend you follow the business systems mantra, "Document what you do and do what you document" when developing and implementing your business system(s). I advise you to resist the "knee jerk" temptation to quickly add steps, procedures, and forms to address an issue before confirming every root cause(s) that led up to your challenge. I suggest you only add additional procedures, forms, etc. as a last resort and as is absolutely necessary, since the sum of all these actions may slow your overall business productivity and efficiency. I also recommend you be aware of people who may want to propagate and/or expand a certain procedure or system just to "make their job easy" and/or add unnecessary bureaucratic *red tape*. It's been my experience that permitting the addition of non-value added procedures without justification may eventually result in your business system "gobbling up" critical resources that can be used to complete more value-added activities.

As a final comment, I recommend you should implement some sort of business system practices and forms within your company to document and ensure compliance to critical procedures and make sure you meet and/or exceed your business goals; I suggest it just makes your business better. What form your business system(s) takes for your company is up to you and sometimes your marketplace—I suggest you choose wisely.

## For More Information and Advice

Please contact us at www.chargeupyourbusinessbook.com and/or www.gbicego.com if you would like more information and advice for your business systems and certifications challenges such as the importance of your business systems and certifications, steps to business system certification, minimum quality procedures and/or any other challenges—we are here to help.

# CHAPTER 7

# PRODUCTION

## The Importance of Production

I recommend your production throughput must always be your third operations priority, after your first employee health and safety and second product and/or service quality priorities—I advise you always follow, as I have, these three priorities in every business operations decision and situation. In fact, I also advise you teach these three priorities to all your employees as I have done for decades. The reasons for these priorities are simple from a business point of view: since your business needs both employees and customers, your health and safety focus takes care of your employees while your quality and production priorities take care of your customers. To put it in another way: your business product and/or service may not be effectively delivered by an injured employee(s) who is not at work or by those remaining employees affected by the serious injury of a co-worker (1st priority), and most customers may be able to accept a slightly late delivery in some cases (3rd priority) but never a bad quality product and/or service (2nd priority).

## Your Schedule

I recommend your production efforts must start with a documented schedule that answers that basic operations question, "What do our customers need, how much of each, and by when?" You may think, "Well, that makes sense; of course, all production initiatives start with a schedule." But you may be shocked how often I start working with a client/company where I quickly confirm there is no formal production plan or schedule. When this is the case, I then ask, "Then how does everyone know what to do?" After which I typically receive a variety of sometimes conflicting answers—no wonder operations activities seem to be in disarray.

Without a formal documented schedule, I suggest your employees are left to produce whatever they need on a day-to-day, or even an hour-by-hour, basis to satisfy those customers, managers, or supervisors who *yell the loudest*—they are forced to follow the philosophy "the squeaky wheel gets the grease." Without a formal documented schedule, your employees may be under constant stress, trying to make everyone happy (which is impossible most of the times), and perhaps unnecessarily wasting more raw materials and increasing process downtimes while completing multiple change overs. Without a formal documented schedule, your production may suddenly come to a halt due to running out of raw materials and/or packaging, there's an unscheduled power outage to repair your transformer, or an upcoming statutory holiday that everyone forgot about. Due to the constant operations chaos caused by the lack of a formal documented schedule, some employee(s) may not show up for work, or just quit, leaving you and your remaining employees wondering why some customers are leaving as well.

I strongly recommend that a basic and compulsory tool for any effective business operation is a simple and effective schedule—it is mandatory in my opinion. I suggest every operations activity inherently revolves around your production schedule and you should always ask, "How will this issue(s) affect our production schedule?" before any decision is considered or implemented. I propose your production schedule does not need to be complicated; in fact, the simpler the better in my experience. I have seen everything from a simple sheet of paper pinned to a wall listing the current and next orders, to a more complex, multi-terminal, multi-location, resource planning system that needs to be administered and managed by an entire separate department(s) of people with a resource planning administrator and small group of schedulers at each location.

I have also witnessed a simple manual scheduling system where people schedule production for each day of the current three-month period on one wall, plan each day's production for the next three-month period on another wall, and forecast each day's production for the following three-month period after that on a third wall. This system uses actual cards to signal all their end product and related components' requirements and runs their entire multi-hundred thousand square foot production facility. They also follow a practice to never deviate on what and how many end product(s) they produce during the entire current three-month period. Depending on your point of view, this system may sound like utopia, or just boring, but in my opinion it is a very efficient scheduling and production system. In the end, I recommend you implement, use, and constantly improve whatever production scheduling system works best for your business.

Here's a personal example of how implementing an effective schedule can help resolve multiple business operations challenges. After assuming responsibility for a company's operations, I soon discovered they had no formal production schedule in place for their twenty plus processing machines. Every week, they would review their customer orders, and then decide what machine should run which order—this informal system seemed to work at least on the surface. I began noticing issues though, such as we were always running out of high-volume raw materials on a regular basis while storing too much low-volume raw materials for too many months. These raw material variances caused internal production problems and frustrated our supplier who sometimes had difficulties keeping up with ever-changing demands. On top of that, our tooling/maintenance people had no forewarnings when machine changeovers would occur and thus were typically unprepared and rushed to complete their tasks while machines and other employees sat idle. It was not too long before I decided we needed a simple but effective production schedule to answer these basic operations questions, "What do we need to make, how much, and by when? What raw materials do we need, how much, and by when? What machine(s) do we need to change over and when?"

My first step was confirming all production tool-machine combinations that were available at any given time and completing a tooling inventory. I then verified the raw material grade and amount required for every product in every tool and compared them to our current BOM (bill of materials) quantities. As an added and unexpected benefit of this exercise, we revised and improved the accuracy of some BOMs and thus raw material ordering quantities. By the way, I recommend you include any raw material wasted/used during changeovers when calculating your total raw material usage. Then I calculated how many parts we could produce for every raw material unit, and how many parts we could produce per shift including raw material unit changeovers. Here's another tip: I suggest you always consider how many raw material unit changeovers are required for each production run and how much time they require when designing your schedule. You may decide to extend a production run in the short term, depending how much time is required for your process to reach *steady state*, and especially if your current changeovers require considerable time and resources. In the meantime, I urge you to begin working to reduce your changeover times to improve your production flexibility and costs. My next step was to *map out* not only all our current customer orders for the following week (which I designated as "firm") but also for the next twelve rolling weeks (which I designated as "forecast") for each and every processing machine.

At first, this exercise seemed like a puzzle at times and required some time to work out, but once I did *figure it out*, all I had to do was maintain it. Another practice I implemented was to "freeze" all customer orders at the end of every Friday and the following week's production schedule. Eventually, the upcoming week's production schedule was completed in little time and prepared for the weekly production meeting attended by all required department heads. Instead of focusing on individual customer orders for a particular product, we banded together multiple customer orders for the same product and ran them as long as possible, taking advantage of fewer processing machine changeovers and scrap. As added benefits, our tooling/maintenance people were provided with a schedule of all upcoming changeovers over the next twelve weeks that met their needs, allowed them to plan what spare parts were required and prepare ahead of time, and resulted in reduced machine changeover downtimes.

Another benefit of this simple scheduling system was the creation of a forecasted raw material usage schedule detailing how much and what raw materials were required at what time, thus quickly correcting past raw material imbalances. In fact, our main raw material supplier began replenishing our warehouse shelves every Friday, ahead of the following week's production requirements. Very soon, we saw our raw material warehouse shelves almost empty on Friday mornings and those same shelves were full on Monday mornings, and empty again on the following Friday. By the way, we always carried a day or so extra inventory in case of weather delays affecting raw material deliveries or other emergencies. I recall our major raw material supplier's representative calling me one day congratulating us on what we've accomplished: consistent weekly firm and forecasted twelve rolling week requirements that did not significantly change on a regular basis. Our supplier told me they have been supplying our company for almost twenty years and have never worked with such steady and consistent weekly requirements, and added they did not know what we did but encouraged us to keep doing it! And as we cycled our raw material inventories more often, we liberated/generated substantial amounts of cash flow and reduced our raw material warehouse space, making it available for other more value-added activities.

As a final note in this personal example, guess what software I used to develop this production schedule with all these benefits? Answer: Microsoft Excel. I recall others suggesting we invest hundreds of thousands of dollars on a resource planning system whose technical support group was located out of the country in a substantially different time zone. While that investigation was proceeding, I developed and we implemented the above simple production scheduling system resulting in substantial benefits with practically no costs.

As you can see from this personal example, we were able to quickly and effectively resolve several operational issues with a simple scheduling system. Another tip: I recommend your scheduling system be flexible enough to handle constant changes, regardless of what format you use. That's one of the reasons I recommend you use Microsoft Excel or visual cards, i.e. you can quickly review various production scenarios and consequences if you are considering to accept a new customer order(s) and how they could affect current orders.

## What if You May Be Late with a Delivery?

What do you if a new or current customer wants to give you a new order? You take it of course! That's the obvious answer, but what if you suspect at the time of order you may not be able to deliver on time? You may be tempted to take the new order anyway, as many people do so and *deal with it later*. I suggest it is unfortunate how many people accept customer orders without consulting their operations people before making delivery promises; I am convinced and suggest this practice is a common cause of late customer shipments and their associated costs. I recommend you always accept any new customer order with the condition that you will confirm delivery quickly and after you speak with your production people. I suggest this simple *rule* will demonstrate integrity to your customer, and will avoid any potential future frustrations with them and internally with your production people.

What should you do if you begin to suspect your business may not meet your customer's delivery expectations and you must deliver no matter what? And worse, what if you suspect that your product and/or service may not meet all your customer's quality expectations and you must deliver no matter what? To call or not to call the potentially affected customer(s)—this is the question. You may be tempted to make your delivery as expected and say nothing to your customer(s) while hoping they will not realize and/or mind if you ship a slightly less-than-expected quality product and/or service. But what kind of message will that send to your customers and employees? My advice is contact your affected customer(s) beforehand and warn them about any potential issue(s) while at the same time notifying them what your business will do to eliminate that issue(s) going forward. I also recommend you contact any affected customer(s) beforehand requesting their permission to postpone or "bump" a pre-confirmed order delivery date. I advise you take these actions for two reasons: 1. they demonstrate how you value your current customer(s) and their business, and 2. it ensures you never surprise your current customer(s) with any quality and/or delivery issue(s)—no one likes "bad" surprises.

On the (hopefully) very rare occasion(s) you may need to contact your customer(s) before needing to make a less-than-expected quality shipment and/or potentially change a delivery date, I suggest only two things may happen: your customer will accept the shipment as is or they will not accept the shipment. You may find that your customer(s) will always appreciate your honesty and your company as a valued supplier—this only improves your business reputation and credibility with them. And you may also find your customer(s) may even accept the shipment as is without hesitation and adjust their process(es) to accept your product and/or service on a temporary basis. And that's an added bonus for you and your business as well.

## Inventory Accuracy

Especially if your business involves manufacturing of a physical product(s), your raw material and finished goods inventories may be your largest financial assets in addition to your building, land, and equipment (if you own them). If this is the case for your business, I recommend you must effectively manage your inventory accuracies in the interest of your company's financial survival. Besides, a lending institution (that may have provided financing for your inventory and/or your business) will typically require you to maintain accurate inventories audited by an outside firm(s) since they may be included as financing collateral.

You may recall past days of (or who knows, you may be currently experiencing) keeping excessive raw material and finished goods inventories. But as interest rates rise and/or other business challenges emerge, many companies realize excess inventories require very precious cash flow, the need for warehouses, security, forklifts, trucks, and people to store and move it all the time—it can be very costly when you think about it. On some occasions though, it may be *profitable* to maintain excess raw material inventories, especially if your business is in a commodity marketplace with raw material costs at recent historical market lows and you project those costs may rise. Or you may be able to resist selling some finished goods at currently low prices in anticipation that their market value will increase in the future. I recommend you speak to your finance people to determine if such a *buy and hold* inventory strategy works well for your business and what its effect(s) are going forward.

Once you have an inventory tracking system and procedures in place to ensure acceptable inventory accuracy, I recommend it is critical that each and every one of your employees follow every inventory procedure at all times. All it takes is one improperly completed transaction by one employee, at one time, to begin throwing your entire inventory system into disarray after you've spent all that time and money to implement an inventory tracking system, purchased any equipment, organized your facility, and trained your people. For example, a mistake in a finished goods transaction may affect your raw materials and work-in-process inventories as well. And if you do not identify and correct any improperly completed inventory transaction(s) immediately, and/or such transactions are duplicated unnoticed, I suggest they act like a "cancer" or a large snowball rolling down a hill, gaining momentum and spreading havoc throughout your entire inventory system. If you reach such a point, I recommend you may need to resort to stopping all operations, complete a partial or full inventory count, and perhaps also suffer the consequences of losses.

I suggest there can be at times, unfortunately, another reason(s) for your inventory's inaccuracies: employee theft or what some people call "inventory shrinkage." I prefer to call it what it actually is: stealing. I am not talking about your employee(s) who inadvertently takes a pen or some other single office supply items from work to home in their pocket or briefcase. And I am not talking about any employee who asks to borrow a tool(s) to use over the weekend and return it the following Monday morning. I am talking about your employees who may be systematically stealing from your business, even in small amounts on a regular basis. I recommend that you, as I have, seriously consider these matters and fire anyone who is caught systematically stealing from your business. If needed, I also recommend considering to announce and then install security cameras throughout your facility to obtain evidence of any employee(s) who systematically embezzles from your business before you fire them. I also advise you may need to contact your local police service to obtain any advice and/or their help to investigate such matters.

Depending on the size of your organization and the importance of inventory accuracy to your business, I recommend you have at least one person or a small team of employees whose job is to ensure excellent inventory accuracies at all times. I suggest you can combine these inventory accuracy responsibilities with related tasks such as shipping and receiving if that is more feasible for your business. From a cost/benefit point of view, you may find that the relatively small investment of even one part-time or full-time employee ensuring inventory accuracies may greatly outweigh past or potential inventory *write off* losses and prevent potential manufacturing, receiving, and shipping mistakes. I recommend your inventory accuracy employee(s) must possess at minimum these characteristics and skills: be detailed oriented, have extensive knowledge of your inventory tracking system and its procedures, be persistent, possess a strong determination to find every issue(s) causing any inventory accuracy, and be able to work well with people. I propose your inventory accuracy employee(s) will identify any incorrect transactions, fix them, and implement procedures and/or train other employees to prevent such recurrences. I also suggest they may even target certain inventory items using an ABC cycle count analysis to confirm their on-going inventory accuracies.

My final recommendation to ensure on-going inventory accuracies is to complete inventory counts. In many businesses, and yours, you may be required to complete at least one annual full inventory count. I also recommend you may need to complete inventory counts more frequently if your business is suffering significant and constant inventory inaccuracy issues. After every inventory count, you typically complete an exception or reconciliation report(s) and use your findings to improve your inventory accuracies and procedures. You may consider conducting your inventory counts during a weekend and pay your employees overtime. I suggest you consider, as have I done, to conduct your inventory counts during the week to emphasize inventory accuracy is everyone's job and responsibility, i.e. not something done on a weekend as an afterthought. Completing your inventory counts in less time, with more available people, and avoiding overtime time costs during weekends are additional reasons to complete your inventory counts during regular, weekday times. You may be able to complete full inventory counts in less than a day, depending on the size of your inventories and how well your business runs its inventory systems. And I recommend you always bring at least coffee and donuts, and lunch/ dinner for all employees working on the full inventory counts—make it fun!

## Bills of Materials (BOMs)

I suggest another important and basic component of your inventory tracking and financial costing systems is accurate bills of materials (BOMs). Essentially, a BOM lists your material components, equipment, labour, and all other steps to manufacture your product and/or service. I have seen, and your company may also list, work-in-process items and utility costs as part of each BOM—I recommend you include whatever items into your BOMs that make sense for your business. When done properly, BOMs instantly reflect your business operations or processing cost concentrations. For example, your overall software design process and cost may highlight your labour costs and cycle times whereas manufacturing a physical product may be primarily comprised of your component costs and their movements. For these reasons, your BOMs are also typically an integral part of your overall resource planning system.

Each BOM typically lists at least all the materials and labour components on different levels, 1, 2, 3, etc. For example, your final product on level 1 may be comprised of several sub-assemblies on level 2, whose components are on level 3, and their sub-components are listed on level 4, and so on. Your work centers representing your pieces of equipment or work stations may also be identified when constructing BOMs, and I recommend you include any packaging required for your product and/or service. I also advise you include any processing and setup scrap when constructing BOMs; if not, you may be confronted with what may seem unexplained variances in your inventory levels.

Similar to inventory accuracy employees, I recommend that your employees who construct and maintain your BOMs must also be detail oriented and diligent to maintain their absolute accuracies at all times. And similar to any inventory inaccuracy, I suggest any BOM item inaccuracy can also quickly cause serious operational and financial issues such as ordering too little raw materials to fulfill your customer orders, leading to dissatisfied customers, or ordering too much raw materials and thus unnecessarily consuming your cash flow.

## Workplace Organization

I suggest the physical neatness and organization of your workplace reflects your personal and your employees' attitudes, morale, pride of ownership, and current state of thinking. In fact, I also suggest you can apply this statement to other areas of your life outside of work such as where you live. I suggest you can improve your business effectiveness, productivity, creativity, attitudes, and performances as you improve your workplace organization. I also propose you can achieve similar results for your life outside of business as you improve your personal life organization. Fortunately, there is an effective strategy or process that will help your business become more organized and reap its associated rewards.

The "5S" philosophy or strategy can be central to your workplace organization initiatives. 5S stands for five Japanese words, *Seiri, Seiton, Seiso, Seiketsu,* and *Shitsuke*, which translate into English respectively as *Sort, Set, Shine, Standardize*, and *Sustain*. Depending on your facility size, you may need to invest one to several days to organize your workplace and/or may need to do so with several teams, each team focusing on their workplace area(s). I recommend you initiate your 5S process by first educating your employees about the 5S philosophy and steps, developing motivation, demonstrating the advantages of workplace organization, and setting goals. Then I suggest you organize your employees into 5S teams.

The first *Seiri* or *Sort* step is perhaps the most dramatic from a visual point of view. You and your employees may be shocked about how much junk has accumulated over time in their work area(s). In this step, you physically tag (typically with a red tag) and remove any items that are not consistently used for the work in that area to another common holding area typically named the *red tag area.* I recommend you and your employees be very aggressive at this point to remove any item that is not normally used to complete any task in their work area(s)—don't worry, you may bring it back later.

The second *Seiton* or *Set* step consists of straightening out the remaining *must-have* items in the work area. At this point, your employees may realize that they can reorganize and improve their work process flow and efficiency. Included in this step is relocating any current red tag items to alternate locations, scrapping them altogether or, as a last resort, reintroducing some back into the work area. *Shadow boards* can be used to organize any tools or other items used in the work area as well.

The third *Seiso* or *Shine* step involves cleaning the entire workplace, including the floor, ceiling, walls, and every piece of equipment and item in the work area. You may need lots of rags, cleaning supplies, and perhaps some paint as well. You may also consider painting your equipment white or some other light colour to easily show any fluid leaks, dust, or dirt accumulations. Similar to your first step, you and your employees may be surprised as to how good your work area looks after a *good cleaning.*

The fourth *Seiketsu* or *Standardize* step is when you regulate each work area with overall company standards. For example, every item common to each work area can be manufactured by the same supplier and colour, work place instructions can be posted in the same manner and at common locations near each work station, and each work area can be identified by a standard sign. The possibilities and extent to which you and your employees standardize your workplace can literally become endless—I suggest you choose a level that makes sense for your business.

The fifth *Shitsuke* or *Sustain* step involves maintaining your workplace organization that you and your employees have worked so hard to develop. I propose this last step is the most critical and typically least effectively implemented element of the entire 5S process. I suggest it is during this last *on-going step* that your workplace organization continues to deliver its many benefits. Your business will cease to enjoy 5S benefits whenever you stop maintaining your workplace organization that you've worked so hard to develop. I recommend that one effective strategy to maintain your workplace organization is to implement workplace organization audits, either during your regular health and safety workplace inspections or separate weekly, daily, or shift 5S audits. I also recommend you collect data and measure how many and how often any issues are discovered during these 5S audits, and then reward your employees accordingly.

The 5S workplace organization process can be implemented in any organization and work environment such as manufacturing, an office, warehouse, hospital, a design studio, natural resources exploration, and retail. For example, you can also arrange your desk drawer items in a template to easily locate them, and you can standardize the location of common items in each desk drawer. You may also want to 5S organize where you live outside of your work place. The potential applications for the 5S philosophy may seem endless.

I suggest the 5S philosophy of workplace organization can be summarized by the following statement: a place for everything and everything in its place. As with many important business initiatives, I recommend you must personally lead your business workplace organization philosophy to ensure it is supported by all your employees at all times—it must become part of your business culture. A final piece of advice: take as many pictures of your work areas as possible before and after your 5S activities to document and celebrate your employees' achievements.

## Data Collection

Some people may think, why even bother to collect and monitor production data? At times, collecting production data may seem to require enormous time and other resources that may be better used to support other more value-added business initiatives. My answer to this question is simple: you cannot improve what you do not measure. I propose your production or throughput data, in addition to other measurables, are lead indicators for your overall business performance.

How should you effectively collect production or throughput data? You may be aware of some simple and perhaps more complicated methods to collect production data. I have seen automated and relatively sophisticated data collection methods using programmable logic controllers (PLCs) that monitor equipment inputs and outputs displaying production throughput on a large electronic sign above machines. I have also observed where you can log into a computer network and monitor production throughput live, minute-by-minute, and generate what seems to be an infinite number of reports. Such automated production data collection methods may be beneficial and/or required for many and your organization, especially for very high level production processes; as with many issues, I suggest you do what makes sense for your business. If feasible for your production process(es), I also suggest you consider implementing a simpler whiteboard strategy as an effective means to collect, monitor, and analyze your production throughput data. You may find using production whiteboards will generate multiple benefits at relatively very low initial and on-going costs.

The *whiteboard method* of data collection consists of a board or easel placed at every workstation on which your employees record and monitor how many total good and bad parts were produced in a particular shift and/or day. This simple data collection tool may initially generate issues within your business as people tend to reveal their personalities once you start holding them accountable for their performance. I also suggest the quality and quantity of the benefits from implementing and using any data collection system will be determined by how well you as a business leader manage various peoples' expectations and reactions to their use. As with many other business initiatives, I recommend your first step to implementing whiteboards or any data collection system is to train your employees about their benefits and how to use them. I then suggest you and your employees quickly develop a whiteboard format and set up a whiteboard at every workstation.

There are various ways to improve the usefulness of your whiteboards to collect your production throughput data. I recommend your most effective whiteboard format is having one page per shift or one page per day showing all shifts with space(s) for employee comments and/or explanation(s) for not reaching any quality and/or production targets. I suggest you can enhance your whiteboard display effectiveness by using different colour markers such as green (for at or above target) or red (for below target) for the number of parts produced. It is also important you regularly monitor that all employees record production data for every hour and/or shift as required—in essence, your whiteboard data will provide a basis for all future production throughput analyses and improvements. As your employees and leaders work with whiteboards, I suggest your business will realize multiple benefits by identifying and resolving numerous safety, quality, and productivity issues, all leading to lower production costs and higher business profits.

As a business leader, you can use production data to identify any issues and correct them as soon as possible. Unfortunately, I have seen at times how some business leaders *abuse* production data collection to criticize or embarrass their employees. I recommend you consider any single, unfavourable data point, depending on its severity, may not be as "bad" as an unfavourable trend—of course there are exceptions such as any critical employee injury. I suggest you consider a single, unfavourable data point, after which your process(es) and employees recover, may not be as significant as an unfavourable trend. So, if your process has a "hiccup" and quickly recovers afterwards, my advice is to resist any initial temptation to over-react (again depending on its severity) and determine if this occurrence was an anomaly that can be or has already been corrected. After a second or any other unfavorable recurrence, you may definitely have an unfavourable trend at which time I recommend you and your team(s) intervene as quickly as possible, depending on the severity of any resulting consequences.

Another critical aspect of data collection is its accuracy. Similar to inventory and BOM accuracies, I propose production data accuracy is essential for you to make good business decisions. In fact, I suggest your data accuracy is actually more important than the data values themselves. You may have needed to address, as have I, situations where people have tried to "fudge the numbers" to look good and/or avoid the consequences of some unfavourable data. I recommend you inform your managers, supervisors, employees, customers, and suppliers that you have zero tolerance for any intentional and/or deliberate data collection manipulations and/or inaccuracies. I also recommend you implement the appropriate disciplinary actions against anyone who deliberately falsifies and/or is negligent when recording and submitting production throughput and other business data.

## For More Information and Advice

Please contact us at www.chargeupyourbusinessbook.com and/or www.gbicego.com if you would like more information and advice for

the your production challenges such as the importance of production, your production scheduling, deliveries, inventory accuracies, bills of materials, workplace organization, data collection and/or any other challenges—we are here to help.

# CHAPTER 8

# MAINTENANCE

## Reactive vs. Preventative Maintenance

Would you knowingly or unintentionally operate a vehicle or any other piece of equipment until it runs out of electricity or gas, or until it catastrophically fails? Should you practically fly a commercial airplane without stopping for fuel, checking that all systems are in good condition, or that the pilots and crew members are in good mental and physical conditions? Does a power plant keep producing electricity without stopping for repairs and upgrades? And can you physically keep walking, running, or swimming without rest? Obvious answers to these questions may be "of course not." Then why do some businesses continue to run their processing equipment until it breaks? And why does it seem there is more time and money available to fix an equipment problem after it occurs (reactive maintenance), but there seemed to be *no time* and *no (less) money* available to do complete, periodic, preventative maintenance tasks that could have prevented such an equipment breakdown(s)?

Equipment breakdowns in a reactive maintenance company may typically start the night before an important facility visit, on a late Friday afternoon after a week filled with many challenges, or just before a long weekend and/or statutory holiday. At that point, you may need to contact and call in additional maintenance personnel, some of which may be unreachable at the moment. After watching your equipment sit idle and waiting some time for additional maintenance people to arrive, they may discover they need some spare parts in addition to what they already have in-house. Subsequently, you may need to contact suppliers who hopefully are willing to leave their families or whatever they are doing to open their stores so your maintenance employees can meet them there to purchase additional replacement parts. Sometimes special "opening fees" may be charged to send a supplier's employee in the middle of the night to open their shop. It may seem like highway robbery at the time, but I suggest you consider paying such "opening fees" if you are in an emergency situation. You may also need to send or receive multiple phone calls, texts, and emails to remain updated with your progress or lack thereof. Is all this pain and, most important, costs, worth it? When your company pursues reactive maintenance practices, I propose Murphy's Law will apply: anything that can go wrong will go wrong.

I suggest preventative maintenance is a key to sustaining your business's efficient and flexible design, and manufacturing and delivery processes to satisfy your customer needs. The opposite of preventative maintenance is reactive maintenance when you subscribe a "fix it when it breaks" philosophy. I suggest practicing reactive maintenance strategies may seem tempting and advantageous in the short term since you may be thinking you are maximizing production throughput and minimizing your operational costs, but my experience tells me you may perhaps delay and create much larger problems in the future. Therefore, I recommend you consider implementing a new, or improving your current, preventative maintenance program. In this chapter, I will present some important ideas and concepts on how you can keep your business equipment running without drastically affecting your delivery processes and operational costs.

## Your Preventative Maintenance Plan

I recommend your preventative maintenance program be driven by your business process or equipment uptime goals. Once your business equipment uptime objectives have been established, I suggest you and your team begin establishing your preventative maintenance plan by first listing all your production pieces of equipment and any material handling equipment such as forklifts, cranes, conveyors, lifting chains, and dollies. I also suggest you include all facility items in your preventative maintenance plan list such as your building roof, your heating, air conditioning, lighting systems, and items such as your main electrical panels, transformers, and air compressors. I also recommend you include any transportation items such as any trucks, trailers, dock levellers and bumpers, all doors, driveways, rail lines, or boat docks. Finally, I propose you include all your office items such as your network server, theft and fire alarm systems, any security cameras, all your desktop and laptop computers, and communications devices such as printers and cell phones in your preventative maintenance plan.

Your second step to develop your preventative maintenance program is to determine what and how often preventative maintenance tasks need to be performed on each item. You may also want to record what preventative maintenance kit or tool(s), e.g. grease, spare part(s), etc., is required for each preventative maintenance task. I also recommend you refer to all the owner's manuals and equipment warranties that should have come with all your equipment to confirm preventative maintenance tasks and frequencies. Hopefully all your equipment owner manuals are filed in one place; if not, I recommend that you have that done as soon as possible and perhaps also electronically scan them as a backup. Your preventative maintenance tasks frequencies may vary from every hour or less, every shift, day to every week, month, quarter, year, or any multiple of these time frames. Rarely can some maintenance tasks be left until something actually fails, such as replacing an expired light bulb—for these tasks, I recommend you have some spare parts available.

Your preventative maintenance plan and schedule can be designed using a variety of formats. I have implemented something as simple as a sign stating "change oil every shift" with a checklist to a more complex preventative maintenance software program and database. These total preventative maintenance software packages not only develop your program and schedules, but may also be used to track your tool crib spare parts inventories. If feasible for your business, you may consider using Microsoft Excel and/or Project to design and monitor your preventative maintenance program and schedules. Always be mindful that an effective preventative maintenance plan and schedule format needs to be flexible enough to easily absorb any changes, additions, deletions, and updates as your team completes each task.

## Who Does Your Preventative Maintenance?

After you've identified and listed all your pieces of equipment and facility items, as well as their associated preventative maintenance tasks and their frequencies, I propose your third step is to assign these tasks to the appropriate person(s). Typically, your maintenance personnel may complete all your preventative maintenance and repair tasks. Or is there anyone else you can assign some preventative maintenance tasks? I suggest you consider assigning some simple preventative maintenance tasks to your employees who regularly use that piece of equipment as part of their job. At first, you and/or your maintenance personnel may think that only they are, or can be, trained and trusted to complete all maintenance and repair tasks—I suggest this philosophy and its benefits are limited.

I recommend you consider implementing a Total Productive Maintenance (TPM) Program and the concept of *autonomous maintenance* within your business. Autonomous maintenance is training and allowing your equipment operators to complete simple adjustments and preventative maintenance tasks on equipment they operate on a regular basis. I suggest implementing autonomous maintenance not only develops your employees' sense of involvement and process ownership, but also makes them more value-added individuals with your company. Your autonomous maintenance strategy may help you avoid hiring additional and typically more expensive maintenance personnel, and may "free up" your current maintenance personnel to focus on larger, more critical preventative maintenance activities.

## When Do You Complete Your Preventative Maintenance?

Typically, preventative maintenance tasks are scheduled during regular equipment downtimes such as changeovers, weekday "off shifts," weekends, and/or during annually scheduled facility shutdowns. I suggest you consider one of your preventative maintenance program goals should be to complete as many preventative maintenance tasks, including those that require hours and/or days, during your business *prime time*, i.e. typically during weekday regular business hours. You may find it very satisfying and beneficial to inform and permit a maintenance person to complete their scheduled preventative maintenance tasks during an upcoming shutdown or changeover scheduled during their regular work shift hours. In this case, your maintenance person or crew will have time to pre-purchase all their required items for their *preventative maintenance kit(s)*. In addition, your maintenance personnel may also have their suppliers available during regular business hours to source any items they discover are required while performing their preventative maintenance tasks.

You may be wondering what to do with some or all of your other employees not involved in preventative maintenance tasks that occur during your business *prime time* hours. I propose the following value-added activities: various health and safety and quality trainings, employee communications meetings, workshops, cycle counts, inventory counts, and workplace organization exercises. If you've exhausted all possibilities, I suggest you allow your other employees to take vacation time or, even better, give them their shift off, if that makes sense.

## Spare Parts

Creating spare parts lists for all your equipment and facility items is another critical part of your preventative maintenance program. An easy and useful way to start your spare parts lists is collecting all your spare parts purchase orders over the past year(s). You can use your spare parts lists and the cost of each item to develop your maintenance budget(s), and I recommend you also include any service call labour costs in your maintenance budget(s).

After you've created your spare parts lists, I propose your next step is to identify which spare parts can be categorized as *critical*. Critical spare parts are those that must be on-site or available on a moment's notice at a nearby supplier's facility to keep your equipment running without excessive downtime(s). Critical spare parts may also be characterized by relatively long lead-times and/or expensive costs. I recommend you identify, purchase and/or design plans to have access to as many critical and non-critical spare parts to minimize your equipment downtimes and ensure the smooth operation of your business.

I also propose you develop and designate a tool crib area to control the storage, use, and replenishment of all your processing and facility equipment spare parts. I suggest you consider maintaining your tool crib under lock and key at times to prevent any, let's say, "permanent borrowing" of spare parts and/or tools. You may also consider hiring a part-time or full-time tool crib attendant who will focus their activities to minimize overall maintenance items costs and prevent multiple people from over-ordering and stocking spare parts throughout your facility. I also suggest you consider the benefits from purchasing and employing a computerized preventative maintenance and/or tool crib database software program to track your spare parts and to create spare parts buying alerts. If the option of a specialized tool crib software is not practical for your business needs, I suggest you consider using alternate methods such as handwritten lists and/or indicators, Microsoft Excel and/or similar software.

I also suggest that you implement and enforce the practice to order and have delivered any replacement spare part(s) before you think you may need it again. You may not believe how often Murphy's Law comes true when you've ordered an additional spare part after you used your last one, and then need the same component(s) before your spare parts order arrives. You may also find it beneficial to order and maintain a certain reasonable level of spare parts that are commonly used in your business processing and facility equipment.

And finally, I recommend that you implement and enforce the practice of purchasing and using as many standardized and readily available spare parts as possible. Standardized spare parts may also complement each other in terms of physical tolerances, sizes, electrical, and other requirements. There may be nothing worse from a repair point of view than trying to fit or "MacGyver together" spare parts made from different manufacturers and/or specifications—you and/or your employees may "pull your hair out" trying to do so.

## Some Final Thoughts on Maintenance

Ensuring your safety, maintenance, and production employees approve or *buy-off* all processing and facility equipment before it is designed, built, and leaves your equipment supplier's facility is one of the best strategies I recommend, and have practised myself, to minimize preventative maintenance costs, repairs, and equipment downtimes. This simple, preventative approach allows any equipment issues to be identified and corrected while the equipment is still in the design or construction phase at your equipment supplier's facility.

I also recommend that you and your employees learn about and implement various methods to forewarn when something is wrong with a piece of equipment and/or process and preventative maintenance is required—this concept is known as *Andon* in lean manufacturing terminology. Such warning methods can be as simple as an indicator light or highlighting a pressure or flow gauge zone denoting when pressure or flow is too low or high. Other forewarning methods include implementing a workstation trouble light and/or walkie-talkies to enhance communications between your operators and maintenance personnel. Another strategy, already discussed, is to paint your equipment white or any light colour to reveal any sign(s) where preventative maintenance may be required, such as fluid leaks and dust/dirt accumulation. You may also find that painting your workplace walls white and/or other light colours will result in a brighter workplace, reduce the amount of electric lighting required, and generally make your employees happier.

If some of these preventative maintenance ideas may seem at first to be "out of the box" or perhaps not feasible for your business, your only alternative is to continue practicing your reactive maintenance strategy. I suggest you will never escape the need to perform maintenance activities on your business process equipment and facility. You either complete preventative maintenance tasks on a regular basis at a relatively lower total cost, or complete reactive maintenance tasks in larger *chunks* on a haphazard basis that may be typically more expensive in total cost, affecting your equipment uptimes and perhaps your safety and quality performances as well. As an auto mechanic said in a 1970s oil filter TV commercial, "The choice is yours. You can either pay me now (less), or pay me later (more)."

## For More Information and Advice

Please contact us at www.chargeupyourbusinessbook.com and/or www.gbicego.com if you would like more information and advice for

your maintenance challenges such as reactive versus preventative maintenance, your preventative maintenance plans and programs, who does your preventative maintenance and when, spare parts and/or any other challenges—we are here to help.

# CHAPTER 9

# SECURITY

## Physical Building / Office Security

There are many options available to secure your business building and/or office such as physical keys, swipe cards, keyless pads with and without fingerprints, up to retinal and other biometric scans. I suggest how much physical security your business requires is dependent on both your business, personal, and your employees' needs. That is, how much security will be required to protect your business, allow you to sleep at night, and permit your employees to feel comfortable while working in your business? I recommend you find a balance between your business, personal, and employees' needs while considering the necessity to protect the privacy of your employees and any visitors to your facility.

As a minimum, I recommend your business physical building and/or office requires both entry or burglar and fire alarms; they may also be required as part of your business insurance policy. As with any system or piece of equipment, it is critical that regular maintenance and testing be performed on your alarm systems to ensure they remain operational at all times. Typically, there is an alarm event *call order list* that your security firm requires from your company. I suggest you assign or "volunteer" employees on your alarm event call list considering their position, trustworthiness, reliability, and proximity to your facility. Typically, a management person who lives closest to your facility and/or has maintenance responsibilities is listed first, followed by other management and trusted employees listed thereafter. I also recommend you implement a practice requiring anyone who is contacted for any alarm event to contact you as well.

If you select a physical key system to secure your business facility, I recommend you use key profiles that may be very difficult to duplicate, and issue as few keys as practically possible. I also suggest you develop and maintain a list of all permanent and temporary key holders, and when they receive and return any key(s). I also advise that each key holder sign a *key use document* emphasizing they are personally responsible for each key issued to them, and they must immediately report if any key is lost, or else possibly face disciplinary actions. I recommend you create a list of all keys and where they are used, purchase and maintain a master key box, and label all keys. I also advise you include regular lubrication of all keyholes as part of your preventative maintenance program.

If you choose a badge or keyless system to secure your business facility, I first recommend that every employee be provided with their own unique security code or badge that is never shared with anyone. I suggest you must make the consequences of sharing security badges and/or codes very clear to all your employees. If, for any unavoidable reason(s), codes or badges are shared and/or compromised, I advise that your employees must immediately inform the appropriate person(s) so that compromised codes can be cancelled and new codes can be issued to each person. I also suggest you implement the procedures and practices outlined for keys in the previous paragraph if you decide to use badges to secure your business facility. Although badges may offer some advantages over keys, I advise that you leave them blank (i.e. do not print your company's or any employee's name on them) in case any badge is lost or stolen, preventing anyone else from using it inappropriately.

## Network / Cyber Security

Unlike physical building or office security, you may find it shocking how some businesses and individuals pay relatively little attention to, and invest comparatively little resources into, their cyber security. It seems too often we hear about some cyber-attack(s) that was conducted against individuals, or a large institution or company, and their data was held for ransom. Or that some large retailer or bank network was successfully compromised where money and/or customer information was stolen, or someone infected a popular software program, or that people can hack into your laptop camera, or some latest malware has been creating havoc around the world. And these are, what I suspect, the relatively few incidents we may be informed about.

In this increasingly digitally connected world we now live in, I strongly recommend it is critical that you have an effective, secure, and up-to-date cyber security program in place for your business and personal life. No longer do thieves and/or your competitors need to physically enter your business facility (if you have one these days) to steal your business secrets—all they need to do is hack into your network database and steal anything or everything they need in one or a few clicks. As with many things in business and life, the internet is so transparent that it can be used for both good and bad intentions.

There are many techniques to improve your network security and protect your business data from both outside hackers and internal personnel with unfavorable motives. As a starting point, I recommend to locate your network server in a secure area far away from other activities and minimize access to that area. I also recommend you ensure that no one has the ability to directly connect to your business computer network from any outside device. You may consider email as an exception to this practice—in this case, I suggest you place all your business emails on a separate server. I also advise you backup all your network data and emails on a regular basis, and have in place alarms and reaction plans in case someone tries to compromise your network. I also propose you purchase and install an email spam filtering software and regularly monitor any activity reports.

I also recommend additional information protection policies and practices such as never store sensitive information and files on a laptop drive in case it may get lost and/or stolen. I advise that all your employees use password protection to access their desktops, laptops and sensitive files. And I recommend that all passwords are composed of capital and small letters, numbers and special characters, and are changed on a regular basis. I also suggest you consider password protecting sensitive files when sending them via email in case they are inadvertently sent to an incorrect recipient. Finally, you may find it beneficial to purchase and maintain cyber-attack insurance for your business.

## For More Information and Advice

Please contact us at www.chargeupyourbusinessbook.com and/or www.gbicego.com if you would like more information and advice for your security challenges such as your physical building/office security, network/cyber security and/or any other challenges—we are here to help.

# PART III – YOUR CONTINUOUS IMPROVEMENTS

# CHAPTER 10

# AN INTRODUCTION TO CONTINUOUS IMPROVEMENTS

## Change

I suggest that many people generally do not like change; in fact, you may know people who seem to do everything possible to resist change. I think resisting change is part of human nature, but that does not mean people cannot and should not change for the better. But everyday reality is full of change. The sun rises every morning and sets every evening—it is in constant motion. The same can be said for the clouds, weather, seasons, all of nature, and people too—all constantly changing.

I suggest that most changes are neutral, i.e. most changes can be interpreted as *good* or *bad*, depending on each person's point of view. For example, different people may perceive the same common change of the seasons from spring to summer, to fall, and to winter in different ways. If a person prefers summer, they may not like the season change to fall and winter, and vice versa. Similarly, when you as the business leader implement a change to a current policy, or execute a new policy, you may find some of your employees perceive that change as "bad," while others may ask, "What took you so long?"

Implementing continuous improvements involves change—there's no way around it. Sure, you and your employees may desire the benefits of, and results from, continuous improvements activities, but many people would rather avoid the mandatory work of changing how they do things in order to generate those benefits and results. I suggest resistance to change is responsible for many lost opportunities and failed businesses. But there are at least three strategies that you can implement in order to facilitate positive changes to help your business grow and prosper.

One key strategy to successfully implementing positive change is consistency, i.e. being consistent when implementing change. This concept may sound like a contradiction because it reflects what I suggest is the reality that most people simultaneously need both change and consistency. Let me explain: since many people resist change, I recommend it is critical that you as the change leader be consistent while implementing every change. For example, you may follow a consistent series of change implementation steps such as brainstorming with individual employees, discussing any future changes during employee meetings, convening separately with employee groups, and then posting a memo announcing the upcoming change implementation date(s). Another change consistency strategy is practising leading by example, i.e. "do what I do, not what I say." I suggest that if your actions and/or decisions as the change leader are inconsistent when implementing changes, even once, your employees may dismiss the new change as another "flavour of the month" or another "management thing that will wear off." Right after that first infraction, skepticism may set in making it even more challenging to implement further change—it's a constant battle like waves hitting a shoreline, constantly back and forth. As a change leader, you can think of yourself as waves hitting a shoreline (your organization) consistently and powerfully as you change your business for the better over time.

A second important strategy to successfully implementing positive change is to do so in steps or in increments. I propose the amount of change in your current *change step* is determined by how well your business will absorb that change and how much impact you want to make on your business at that time. At the beginning of your business continuous improvement journey, you may consider to implement smaller changes and then execute larger changes as your people become accustomed to change(s). Or you may decide on a strategy to first implement an initial large change(s) to shock your business, followed by a smaller change to allow your people to become accustomed to your first change(s), and then by another series of changes with increasing amounts of change afterwards. Many organizations cannot absorb substantial changes while other companies need to implement as much change as soon as possible just to survive. I recommend determining the amount and frequency of implementing positive changes is perhaps one of your most important roles as a business leader—it requires experience, some intuition, and faith that what you're doing is appropriate to ensure your long term business success.

A third and final important key to implementing positive change is to avoid changing anything and/or everything just for the sake of change. Sometimes you may encounter a policy, practice, or method that works, as is. If an existing practice or method is working well, I suggest you consider that it may have passed the *test of time* and probably has already been tweaked, changed, modified, and optimized to a point where any further investment of time or resources will result in diminishing returns. If this is the case, my recommendation is to leave that time-tested policy, practice, or method alone, and focus your business continuous improvement efforts and activities to other practices that need to be improved.

## Continuous Improvement Methodologies

There may seem to be so many continuous improvement method-ologies available to implement positive changes within your business that you may not know where to start. Such methodologies include World Class Manufacturing, Reengineering, Six Sigma, Total Quality Management, Lean, Kaizen, Toyota Production System, and ISO 9000.

I suggest, as you learn about and investigate each of these continuous improvement methodologies, you may find that several/many of them share similar strategies and tools to achieve their common objective of positive continuous improvements. You may have listened to and participated in what seems like endless debates about which methodology(ies) is/are best for your business. I recommend you obtain advice about which overall methodology best suits you, your business, and employees, and then implement that one general methodology. Or you may develop your own unique overall continuous improvement philosophy by implementing a variety of tools from an assortment of other continuous improvement philosophies. I recommend you consider Kaizen or Lean Manufacturing as your overall methodology to achieve your business continuous improvement goals.

*Kaizen* is a Japanese word that combines two words meaning *change for the better*. This is a critical point because change initiated just for the sake of change is not always better, as I have already discussed in the previous section. Kaizen's origins are rooted in the commonly accepted history that Japanese companies embraced and improved upon the idea of *zero defect production*, devised by Dr. Deming, to improve the quality and reduce the costs of their products and services. It is also commonly accepted that Kaizen and the Toyota Production System were developed through the collective works of people such as Masaaki Imai, Shingeo Shingo, Taiichi Ohno, Genichi Taguchi, Kaoru Ishikawa, and many others.

There are many techniques or tools within Lean and/or Kaizen such as PDCA (plan-do-check-act), SDCA (standardize-do-check-act), 5-Whys, 5S (sort, set in order, shine, standardize, sustain in English), fishbone diagrams (for root cause analysis), Kanban (scheduling system with cards/visuals), One-Piece Flow, OEE (overall equipment effectiveness), TPM (total productive maintenance), Andon (visual/audible alerts to process problems), and so on. Each one of these topics can be expanded into its own program and initiatives designed to improve the overall quality, cost, and delivery of your business products and/or services.

For example, OEE (Overall Equipment Effectiveness) is a process measure considering its availability, throughput, and quality performances. In its formula form, OEE (overall equipment effectiveness) = A (Availability) x T (throughput) x Q (Quality). Your process Availability % is a measure of its availability to produce parts and is equal to the amount of a process uptime divided by the total available time. Your process Throughput % is a measure of its speed and is equal to the number of parts (both good and bad) produced times the ideal cycle time divided by the total operating time. Your process Quality % is a measure of the process yield and is equal to the number of good parts divided by the total number of parts produced. As you collect data, determine and chart your process OEEs, you may initially find that your process performance(s) is below a commonly recognized target of 85%—if this is your situation, do not despair. I suggest the rate of your improvements may be more important, rather than your first actual OEE results, during the initial stages of your company continuous improvement journey as you focus on reaching your OEE target(s). I also suggest you may eventually witness improvements in the overall quality, cost, and delivery of your products and/or services as you improve each of the three OEE component measures for every business process.

Another important Kaizen philosophy is the idea of *muda* or waste; I recommend that you and your employees must continuously pursue the identification and elimination of all types of waste. *Muda* or waste can be categorized into seven classes within the Kaizen philosophy. Transportation waste occurs when you unnecessarily move items, while inventory waste occurs when you process and store too many components or finished goods. Defects waste occurs when non-acceptable parts are produced from a process. Motions waste occurs when someone performs unneeded movements to complete a task whereas waiting waste occurs when you unnecessarily wait for a task to be completed. Finally, over-production waste occurs when you produce more products than are required, and over-processing waste occurs when more work is done to a product than as required. Once you've trained yourself and your employees to recognize these seven types of waste, I suggest you may be amazed as to how much waste or *muda* is contained within your current business processes and the almost limitless opportunities you have to implement continuous improvements within your company.

Employee involvement is perhaps the foundation of your Lean/Kaizen and any continuous improvement program. I cannot stress and advise you enough about how critical the involvement of your employees is to the success of every improvement initiative. As much as this idea makes sense intellectually, you may find for some reason(s) many employees feel their ideas are never, or rarely, solicited and, if they are, they are rarely, or never, implemented. I recommend unleashing your employees' ideas is perhaps the best thing you can do for your business, your employees, and your customers. Think about it: who is more experienced or knows more about a certain task, equipment, or process, at least from an operational point of view, than that person(s) who spends most of their work time completing that task?

Considering this above fact, why does it seem at times that those employees who are most involved with a process are typically one of the last people consulted about changes to that process, if they are consulted at all? Personally, over eighty percent of the ideas my teams and I have implemented originated from direct-line employees who worked with those processes/equipment day in and day out. In most cases, I suggest your direct-line process employees may have many ideas to improve their processes but may not have the time or resources to implement changes to their processes. I strongly advise you utilize that typically untapped wealth of continuous improvement ideas from all your employees. Your employees, in addition to your customers and perhaps suppliers, may hold the secret(s) to your business's long term success.

## Your Continuous Improvement Priorities

The best operations continuous improvement advice I can offer you as a business leader is to constantly focus your attention, time, and efforts to improve these six priorities: safety, quality, delivery, continuous improvements, employee morale, and costs. You may realize that I have dedicated various chapters in this book on the topics of safety, quality, production (or delivery), and continuous improvements—this is not a coincidence. The topics of employee morale, leadership, people, communications, human resources, and change are further discussed in my other book, *Charge Up Your People!: 27 Ways to Boost Performance.* You may consider these six priorities as the sources of most or all of your unbudgeted costs that reduce your forecasted profits. Therefore, you may increase your business profits as you improve your business safety, quality, delivery, continuous improvements, employee morale and cost performances – this is one of the key themes for this entire book. These six priorities or elements are intertwined throughout your organization, and your mastery of each and everyone one of them is critical to your long term business success. Let me explain in the following paragraphs how these elements may affect your business—strictly from a cost (and profit) point of view.

**Safety:** If an employee(s) becomes injured, you must obviously ensure they are taken care of and recuperate as quickly as possible. As a result of any employee injury, your business may need to run overtime to make up for lost production (this costs money) and/or their absenteeism (that costs money too). You may also need to hire additional people while paying your injured employee their wages/salary (costs more money). You may need to repair and/or improve your equipment and/or facility contributing to the accident (more money), complete any labour ministry orders (more costs), and perhaps even pay additional worker safety insurance premiums (even more money). Poor safety may unnecessarily harm your employees and increase additional business costs, whereas good safety will benefit your employees and business.

**Quality:** If your product and/or service quality suffers, your business may incur additional rework (added costs) and/or may have produced scrap (more money). Your business may also need to run overtime (more costs) and/or use more raw materials as costed for the job (even more costs). Your worst-case quality scenario may occur when you lose a customer(s) due to a quality issue(s). It's almost impossible to accurately estimate the cost to your business reputation, future sales, revenue, and profits when you lose a customer due to bad quality. Poor quality may unnecessarily increase your business costs, while good quality benefits your business, your customers, and your employees.

**Delivery or Production Throughput:** If your business is late delivering any order, you again may need to run overtime (more costs). Similar to quality, your worst-case delivery scenario may occur when your business loses a customer(s) due to a late delivery(ies)—even more costs. Poor delivery(ies) may unnecessarily escalate your business costs, while good delivery benefits your business, your customers, and your employees.

**Continuous improvements:** If you and your employees do not continuously look for cost reduction opportunities and implement improvements, I suggest your business cost structure will "naturally" increase and become uncompetitive over time. With an increasing cost structure and/or less sales, I suggest your business may suffer from one or both of these inevitable results: survive short term with lower or no profits, or become insolvent. A lack of effective continuous improvement initiatives may unnecessarily raise your business costs, while implementing them benefits your business, employees, customers, shareholders, and perhaps suppliers.

**Employee Morale:** Discussed at much more length in another one of my books *Charge Up Your People!: 27 Ways to Boost Performance*, I propose your employee morale is a lead indicator of not only the other five continuous improvement priorities but also for your overall business performance. If your employee morale is suffering, you may be assured that your employee safety, your product and/or service quality, and delivery will soon deteriorate thereafter, thus driving up your overall business costs. Happier, motivated employees may contribute to, and are required for, your business success, whereas miserable employees may eventually lead to your business failure.

**Costs:** I hope you are considering by now that if you focus your attention, time, and efforts on the previous five continuous improvement priorities of safety, quality, delivery (or production throughput), continuous improvements, and employee morale, you may make significant progress to avoid incurring unnecessary additional costs, increase your profits and ensure your long term business success. Besides the five continuous improvement priorities already mentioned, there are always other cost avoidance or cost saving opportunities in purchased items and services, freight, insurance, utilities, and so on—the list is almost limitless. I recommend you make every business decision considering the costs, risks, consequences, and benefits associated with each option.

## Your Employee Continuous Improvement Program

There are so many different employee continuous improvement program formats and tools. I advise you implement an employee continuous improvement program that works for your business and employees. You may also consider modelling employee continuous program ideas, formats, and tools from other sources, and I recommend you modify them for your specific business. Regardless of your program format, I suggest there are at least five requirements for every effective employee continuous improvement program.

The first, and perhaps most crucial, part of your effective employee continuous improvement program is that you as the business leader must personally drive the program, its trainings, and all associated activities, i.e. lead by example and/or drive it *from the top*. As a business leader, I recommend you use your authority and influence to motivate, convince, and/or "sell" your employees to understand and accept the advantages of a continuous improvement program. I recommend you need to ensure all your employees appreciate the importance of continuous improvement for the long term success of the business and eventually their own job security. I also suggest you consider hiring an outside consultant(s) for the early phases of your employee continuous improvement program to perhaps act as another credible source of information and/or change agent. An outside consultant will also ensure you and your employees start off on the right foot by offering to teach and demonstrate the basic principles and tools behind every successful continuous improvement program. An outside consultant can also train one of your employees to continue leading your continuous improvement over the long term.

The second element of your successful employee continuous improvement program is a method(s) used by every employee to identify potential improvement opportunities and submit their idea(s) to improve their work processes. You can design and implement an *ideas form* that each employee will use to describe a problem(s) and their proposed solution(s) to that problem(s). Besides their name, date of submission, and location of the opportunity, I suggest you leave adequate space on your *ideas form* for your employees to describe the problem(s) and their potential solution(s)—even leave room for them to draw a sketch(es) of the problem and their solution.

The third component of your employee continuous improvement program is the process by which all employee *idea forms* are reviewed and acted upon. You may consider to follow a common practice of establishing a small committee to review all *idea forms* deciding each idea's validity and feasibility. On the other hand, I recommend you consider permitting the implementation of any employee idea(s) that does not affect the fit, form, or function of any product and/or service and does not interfere with any customer requirement. I recommend that you first thoroughly train and educate your employees what is meant by affecting your product and/or service fit, form, or function and any other customer requirement before implementing this practice. After adequate initial training and setting up parameters and/or criteria, I suggest you may encourage your employees to immediately implement their own ideas without a committee review within clearly established limits. Implementing this practice will foster employee involvement and demonstrate your trust in your employees' actions. Or perhaps you may consider implementing this practice at a later date after initially working with the committee-review process to review your employee *idea forms.*

The fourth component of your employee continuous improvement program is compensation. Despite the numerous benefits realized from a formal continuous improvement program, I also recommend it is necessary to offer some sort of compensation to ensure your employees' participation. There are many ways to compensate your employees for their involvement and ideas: some companies award a set amount of money after an idea is implemented or for just submitting an idea. Other businesses award a percentage of the resulting cost savings for one year after an idea is implemented. These compensation methods may seem attractive to some, but they may also have some unintended negative consequences. If you prefer to avoid an "ideas for cash" mentality, I suggest you consider a points awarding compensation system. In such a system, you award a point for every idea submission, regardless if the idea is implemented or not, to encourage participation from all your employees. You award an additional point(s) depending if the idea is implemented and/or the extent of improvements is realized by the idea. For every point you award an employee for every idea submission, you may also consider awarding a point to the employee's supervisor to further encourage participation. Points can be then be redeemed for various items of their choice where each item is assigned a certain point value. Some companies rank and acknowledge employees who have submitted the most ideas within a certain period of time. Once again, I recommend you do what makes sense for your business and your employees, keeping in mind that your continuous improvement program compensation strategy goal is to encourage employee participation.

The fifth and another critical requirement for your employee continuous improvement program's long term success is the policy and practice that your employees are not laid off due to improvements associated with your program. Trust me, your employee continuous improvement program may come to a sudden and permanent end soon after the first occasion when any employee(s) is laid off as a result of an idea and/or exercise associated with your program. Even if you "bring back" any employee initially laid off due to an idea and/or exercise associated with your employee continuous improvement program, you have already lost the trust of your employees. I propose your employee continuous improvement program long term success is founded upon your employees' trust that their ideas will never result in anyone losing their jobs. Without this requirement, your employee continuous improvement program success may be limited and eventually doomed to fail, and your business may never reap its associated rewards. While you may need to lay off employees for other reasons, I recommend you always ensure no one perceives any layoffs and/or terminations are the results of any idea(s) implemented through your employee continuous improvement program. Employees whose jobs may have been displaced as a result of an employee continuous improvement program idea(s) can replace any temporary employees you may have, be re-employed in inventory control, 5S, shipping, receiving, administration, training, and/or other value-added activities. Hopefully your business will increase sales as you become more competitive as a result of your employee continuous improvements program, and your previously displaced employees will support your new sales.

## For More Information and Advice

Please contact us at www.chargeupyourbusinessbook.com and/or www.gbicego.com if you would like more information and advice for your continuous improvement challenges such as change, continuous improvement methodologies, your continuous improvement priorities, your employee continuous improvement program and/or any other challenges—we are here to help.

# CHAPTER 11

# YOUR CONTINUOUS IMPROVEMENT STRATEGIES

## Measurables

How do you know if you're on track to achieve your continuous improvement and business goals? The answer is simple: decide which business measurables to track, collect data, and then chart your data to review your measurables trends. You may already have some obvious business measurables such as profit, sales, revenue, market share, and others such as your materials, labour, and overhead costs. I recommend you consider also monitoring your safety, quality, production, delivery, continuous improvement, and employee morale measurables to ensure your business performance progresses over time.

I propose your business measurables can be divided into two categories: primary and secondary indicators. Primary indicators are *higher* or macro level measurables such as your profits and sales whereas secondary indicators are *lower* or micro level measurables such as overtime and scrap. I suggest you set up your business system measurables such that your secondary indicators, typically available on a daily or more short-term basis, can act as early warning signs for your primary indicators. I also recommend you assign a person(s) to coordinate the collection, generation, and updating of charts, and publication of all your business measurables to the appropriate person(s).

You may have some reservations about sharing some or all business measurables with some of your employees. You may be wondering how your employees will react having knowledge of certain data and/or measurables. Could some employees try to take some sort of advantage by being aware of some data or measurables? Could other employees even share some measurables with people outside your business? If you lead a public corporation, this concern may be relatively insignificant since you must report certain business performance measurables and data by law. But if you are leading a private company, it is understandable that this question of what, how much, with whom, and how often to share business measurables with your employees may have more serious consequences and/or implications.

In the private company scenario, I understand both "sides" of the argument. On one hand, I recommend you never allow others, outside of a few trusted advisors, become familiar with your intimate business financial details since it may fall into your competitors' hands and may be used against you and your business. I also suggest at times what may seem like "huge" profits may cause your employees to expect unreasonable increases in wages and/or benefits. Or, what may seem like large losses may cause some employees to start looking for employment elsewhere and/or quit for fear that the company is in serious financial trouble. On the other hand, I suggest you consider that sharing measurables with your employees showing how well the business is or is not progressing, demonstrates how you value their contribution and trust them with such data. I also suggest sharing business measurables with your employees will also make them feel "part of the company," and encourage them to continue acting for the benefit of the company. I recommend you share as many business measurables in as much detail(s) as possible with your employees to gain their trust and support while satisfying your own comfortable level. I suggest the more measurables and details you share with your employees, the more they will be involved in caring about the welfare of the business. In the end, both you and your employees derive livings from the success of the business.

To be effective, I recommend your business measurables need to be simple, understandable, and meaningful to their audience. I propose you may find that your employees are mostly interested in business measurables that they can affect in their own day-to-day work activities. I also recommend you design your business indicator charts with simplicity and colours, e.g. a red-yellow-green speedometer, thermometer, calendar, something that *fills* up or is updated on a daily or weekly basis. I suggest line graphs and/or bar charts can also be used to track your business measurables over a longer time duration such as weeks, months, or years, and perhaps you can use different colours for different teams and shifts.

I also recommend you consider summarizing all your business measurables on a single-page scorecard, especially if you run multiple divisions within the same business to compare their respective indicators and create some competition. You can summarize and compare business measurables amongst various shifts and/or departments within the same division to create some *friendly* competition among your employees. In order to raise the level of awareness or importance of certain business indicators, I suggest you consider determining part or all of any employee wage/salary increases and bonuses to improvements of your key business measurables.

Above all, I strongly advise it is critical that all input data and resulting business measurables or results be accurate. I recommend that you, as have I, may at times forgive people for bad results and encourage/ look forward to their improvement(s). But I also recommend that you, as I also have, severely discipline any employee(s) who has submitted, skewed, and/or falsified any input data, thus producing inaccurate results. I suggest at times the result value may not be as important as the result accuracy; I advise it is far more beneficial to have an accurate *bad* result(s) than an inaccurate *good* result. It's like actually operating a car on a near-empty tank of gas/electrical charge, but the fuel gauge shows full—very quickly and suddenly your car will stop and you won't know why. As discomforting as *bad* accurate results are, I suggest it is better to deal with *bad* accurate results than temporarily deal with *good* inaccurate results. All your business decisions must be based on data and facts that are as accurate as possible.

## Go to Where the Work is Done

Another important, but at times ignored or dismissed, continuous improvement strategy is *go to where the work is done*. That is, I recommend that you as the business leader and your leadership team should actually visit your *front-line* employees to help identify any issue(s) and implement improvements. In addition, I suggest you consider actually becoming trained and learn first-hand what your employees do and how they do it. I propose this strategy will accomplish at least two objectives: 1. it will demonstrate to your employees that you are sincerely concerned about them and their day-to-day issues, and 2. it will provide you a unique viewpoint and accurate data/information about any process issues. As a business leader, I have been trained by my employees and learned first-hand about their jobs and equipment issues for decades, even before any popular television reality show(s) aired showing senior executives working undercover with their employees. I found my first-hand experience provided me a new perspective on, and knowledge about, our business process(es) and helped me make more effective business decisions; I recommend you consider doing the same and gaining similar benefits. I recall a conversation with a business leader whose facility was visited by a world renowned continuous improvement pioneer/leader who asked him only one question in his office, "How many times a day do you go out to your production floor?" When the business leader embarrassingly replied, "Not very often," he learned the valuable lesson that every successful business leader should visit the *front line* as often as possible—I advise you do the same. Below is a personal experience demonstrating the importance and benefits of *going to where the work is done.*

I assumed responsibility for directing a company where I found a critical process had degraded to the point where it typically produced one-third to one-half of its original and designed throughput. I initially solicited the ideas and opinions from my production employees, supervisors, managers, maintenance, and engineering employees, detailing all the process issues and reasons why it was not possible to resolve any of them. In essence, I was told we should remain satisfied with the process's current low throughput. I decided to invite one of the maintenance personnel to run this process with me on a Sunday morning, since it was occupied full-time Monday to Saturday, barely producing enough product to satisfy customer demands. After being trained and running this troublesome process myself, we developed an action plan that I began implementing first thing the next Monday morning. Within several days/a few weeks, we successfully increased process output up to seventy-five to ninety percent of its original and designed throughput on a consistent basis. About a week after that Sunday when I operated that equipment and began implementing our throughput improvement initiatives, I was called to meet with the business owner (my boss) upon their return from an out of town trip. I was asked, "Guess what I just did?" I naturally replied with some curiosity, "What did you do?" They replied, "I just hired the most expensive machine operator in the history of our industry!" and then curiously inquired why I was actually operating machines versus directing others to do so. After we shared a laugh together, I explained how I achieved at least three objectives: 1. everyone will now "think twice" about trying to "pull the wool over my eyes" whenever I ask any question, 2. I demonstrated I was not afraid to "get my hands dirty", and 3. we began witnessing significant throughput improvements on a consistent basis. They were impressed! I suggest at times the saying "if you want a job done right, do it yourself" may be valid, especially when you practise the *go to where the work is done* continuous improvement strategy.

I also recommend you urge your business leadership/management people to visit your business *front line(s)* just as you do. I suggest one of your business management's critical responsibilities is to support your other front-line employees and their work. So what better strategy is there to meet this critical responsibility than to actually going to where the work is done? To expand on a previous statement, over eighty percent of the ideas I and my teams have implemented over the decades originated from employees who worked on those processes day-in and day-out, and from my own personal experiences being trained, working in, and visiting those same processes. I suggest your direct-line employees may have many ideas to improve their processes but not the time and/or resources to implement them. And in most cases, your processes employees may not be able to see you at any time(s) with their improvement ideas during their work time(s), but you and your management team have more flexibility and opportunity to go see them.

I recall another personal experience when I assumed the leadership of an engineering and continuous improvement department. I quickly realized that some of my team members were trained by my predecessor and were satisfied with working on continuous improvement ideas with very little interaction with the production floor employees that would be directly affected by their initiatives. After unsuccessfully persuading some of them to *go where the work was done* on a regular basis, I announced that part of their overall performance review results will be determined by how often they physically *go to where the work is done*. In fact, I even suggested to move their desks from our current office area to the production floor if they did not go to where the work is done. Soon after, and within my first month "on the job," I was summoned to the business leader's office to hear anonymous complaints from some of my team members about my tactics to drive my "WordPerfect" engineers from their office desks to the production floor. His response: "Keep going!" Within a few weeks of starting this practice of *going to where the work is done,* we witnessed increases in the quality and quantity of implemented continuous improvement ideas resulting in more efficient processes and reduced costs.

## Process Mapping

The goal of process mapping is to identify and categorize those process steps that are value-added (you keep those) and non-value added (those you eliminate or reduce). The end results of the process mapping continuous improvement strategy are typically faster cycle times, less inventory, and sometimes less tasks and less people, all leading to reduced operations costs if done properly. As I've already mentioned, I suggest it is critical how you deal with any employee(s) whose job may have been displaced as a result of process mapping or any other continuous improvement strategy. Process maps may come in all shapes and sizes; I recommend you and your team develop simple process maps unless they do not provide a desired result(s) and/or benefit(s).

The process mapping methodology can be summarized in a few basic stages:

1. document every step of your process and what occurs at every step – I recommend to include transportation, work in process, storage, rework, and other steps as required
2. record the time duration of each process step
3. analyze each process step to determine if it is value-added or non-value added
4. eliminate or reduce as many non-value added steps and/or their time durations as possible.

I recommend you include as many employees as possible in a process mapping exercise such as those working in shipping/receiving, production, quality, etc. to ensure no process steps are missed and to foster employee involvement. Once you've completed the second step, you may conclude (as I have numerous times when leading process mapping exercises) that your product spends most of its time being stored, transported, or involved in some other non-value added activity. Your conclusion that your most of product and/or service process time is non-value added is typical—that's the good news! With your recent process mapping information, you and your team(s) can now effectively implement process initiatives that may result in dramatic and impressive improvements. Let me demonstrate with a personal experience of how process mapping can improve your operations efficiencies and costs.

While leading a process engineering department, I began developing process maps for each product line within our manufacturing floor. Focusing on one particular product line, the manufacturing process commenced with raw materials being received and stored in our warehouse for some time. Then these raw materials were distributed to various work stations where they were altered and made into sub-assemblies. These sub-assemblies were then stored on portable dollies that were used to transport them to final assembly. At the final assembly work station, all components were put together, the product was tested, packed, and placed onto a skid, and subsequently placed in a finished goods warehouse where it was stored for weeks or months until it was required for shipment. Excluding the raw material and finished good warehouse storage times, I recall the product required days to process from the first to the last manufacturing step and travelled over thousands of feet! Our plant size was over a hundred thousand square feet, so you can imagine how often these components criss-crossed the entire length of the plant.

After identifying the non-value added steps, we began devising and implementing a plan to relocate all the interrelated work stations closer together, resulting in immediate work in process and process cycle time reductions. We also improved our product quality, reduced our rework by eliminating various transportation and storage defect causes, and concluded we could produce more product with less people. Those employees whose jobs were displaced by this exercise were immediately redeployed in other areas of the company. In the end, we had reduced the total cycle time from days to a few hours (less than one shift), and total process length from several thousand feet to a few hundred feet, while maintaining most of the original employees. Notice that in this process mapping exercise, as with most cost improvement projects, the majority of the cost savings resulted from process times, space, and inventory reductions.

You may be wondering what to do with all the "new" floor space you've freed up as a result of your process mapping exercise(s). Before deciding what to do with your extra floor space, I recommend (as I have done) you segregate or *chain off* this floor space so no one else can use it. Trust me, your material handlers may use this and any "free" space you give them. I suggest you may have several options with this "new/extra" floor area, such as temporarily renting it as storage space to another business to generate some additional business revenue, or make room for an additional revenue-generating process, thus avoiding expenses of renting or buying any off-site space. Your "new/ extra" empty floor space can also serve as a reminder to all your employees about the good work that was done to achieve optimized processes through process mapping. I also recommend , as I have done, you post a huge "open for new business" sign over this floor space and parade every sales person past this area, telling them they need to obtain additional (and profitable) business.

## Automation

Similar to the question to share or not share business measurables, you may often wonder about another continuous improvement strategy: to automate or not to automate? You may know business leaders who became convinced that a new piece of equipment would result in annual cost savings and improved profits. In reality, that expensive piece of equipment arrived late at a higher total cost than quoted, and may not have functioned as well as promised, or not at all. Then I suggest the real fun and games start: the "blame game," and the "I told you so." Everyone seems to have an excuse(s). My advice is you consider to automate a process to whatever extent/level makes sense and be careful not to *over-automate.*

*Over-automation* occurs when an attempt to mechanize what at first seems like a simple task, eventually ends up with trying to implement a series of more complex methods that do not work as well as the original task. Some businesses *over-automate* a task with the goal of labour cost savings, only to eventually keep and move those same employee(s) from performing that original task to subsequently fixing or adjusting what that *over-automation* could not do as well. Many companies may discover, after they've implemented some sort of automation, that any slight variance(s) in their process inputs cannot be absorbed by their new automated piece of equipment, causing it to shut down or, worse, damaging their product(s). In the end, some businesses may waste all this time and money but may still need to keep their employees. And it may get worse: depending on the complexity of their new automated equipment, some businesses may also need to hire additional part-time or full-time technician(s) to keep it operating—and the technician(s) typically costs more than a regular employee(s).

When considering to invest in any automation project, I recommend you and your team ensure that none of your process inputs vary to an extent that they may cause issues for your new piece of automation equipment. For example, a single robot may be adept at performing certain repetitive lifting tasks better than two people, but it may not possess some advantages of human eyes and judgement. I am aware robotic vision systems are continuously improving, but sometimes they may not be as skilled as a human being to adapt to the realities of your process(es). I also recommend you consider and/or budget for any technical help, repair, and maintenance costs associated with any automated piece of equipment. After considering these additional automation costs in our robot example, you may find that adding a manual lift device that can be operated by only one person may actually be more effective and less expensive than replacing two people with a robot.

As discussed in an earlier chapter regarding change, you may find it more efficient and less expensive overall (in terms of purchase costs, overall downtime, and effects on production and product quality) when you automate a large extensive process in stages rather than all at once. I also suggest an added benefit of this step-by-step automation approach is that you have an opportunity to incorporate lessons learned from the previous automation phase(s) into the next one(s).

I also recommend you involve your employees in any automation initiative, especially those whose jobs will be affected by that automation project. You may find some natural resistance from employees at first, depending on how much the new automation will affect their current job(s). Regardless, I recommend you seek your employees' ideas and cooperation as much as possible to maximize the chances of a successful automation project implementation.

## Research & Development

While measurables, process mapping, and automation can be continuous improvement strategies, critical for the relatively short-term success of your business, I suggest your research and development efforts may play a key role(s) in your business's relatively long-term business success. Every successful business actively leads and/or participates in research and development—think of Amazon, Apple, Tesla, Google, General Electric, Bayer, Ford, and any other successful company. I propose every successful business leader understands the value of research and development, and ensures that some portion of their overall budget is dedicated to this critical long-term continuous improvement strategy; I recommend that you do the same.

You may be concerned and/or have some of your employees express concern(s) that investing in long-term research and development projects may be a waste of time, money, human, and other resources, especially if there seem to be no significant and usable results. This viewpoint may seem valid in the short term. To mitigate such concerns, I recommend your business take full advantage of any and all government-sponsored research and development programs where funds or tax credits may be awarded to support your company's research and development efforts and costs. You may find it feasible to hire a consultant to help guide your business through the application and submission processes in order to take full advantage of available government program grants and tax credits. I also recommend you formally track all your research and development projects, and all their associated costs, to provide support for your applications and submissions.

One final piece of advice regarding your research and development efforts: if feasible, I recommend you hire, retain, and motivate the most creative people that you can find for your research and development program and projects. I suggest your research and development employees must be different than all your other (but just as valuable) employees who perform other business activities on a daily basis. Your research and development employees must naturally "think out of the box," and be given extensive latitude to allow their creative thinking processes and ideas to become realities even if there is no practical use for them. Your research and development employees should not be deterred by multiple failures, and should be personally curious and driven "to find out why" something happened or did not happen. I also recommend you provide your research and development employees with their own work area(s), own equipment, and physically segregate them from your other business processes and employees, if feasible (physically off-site at another facility is ideal). At the same time, I suggest you do not deny your research and development employees to interact with your other business operations and employees.

## Your Lessons Learned Database

You may have heard the quote, "Those who cannot remember the past are condemned to repeat it." I suggest this quote is valid, especially in business. If your employees do not learn from past mistakes and experiences, they will be prone to repeating them over and over again, sometimes to your business's detriment. In life, we can read books or access the internet to remember the past and learn from other people's mistakes and experiences. In your business, I recommend you establish and maintain a *lessons learned* database to document any and all issues specific to your company. Your *lessons learned* database is a summary of all your business challenges, problems, failures, and your solution(s) to each of them, and can provide a foundation for future successes.

I recommend you consider your business lessons learned database as important as your business financial statements since it may contain proprietary information that may give your business a competitive advantage(s) in your marketplace(s). I also suggest you consider limiting access to your overall business lessons learned database, e.g. perhaps certain employees from certain functional areas within your business can only access certain sections of the overall database. In addition, you may also consider blocking attempt(s) to print or copy any section(s) of your overall business lessons learned database to prevent any unauthorized distribution of proprietary information.

I recommend your business lessons learned database be organized by sections such as safety, quality, production throughput, maintenance, continuous improvements, research and development, marketing, sales, finance, human resources, etc. I also recommend you require regular updates of your business lessons learned database. For example, ensure your business lessons learned database is updated any time an employee completes an accident investigation report, or implements a solution to address an issue identified in failure mode error analysis. I also recommend you implement standard practices to review your lessons learned database before commencing any project and to update your lessons learned database at the end of every project.

## For More Information and Advice

Please contact us at www.chargeupyourbusinessbook.com and/or www.gbicego.com if you would like more information and advice for your continuous improvement challenges such as measurables, go to where the work is done, process mapping, automation, research and development, your business lessons learned database and/or any other challenges—we are here to help.

# ABOUT THE AUTHOR

Giorgio Bicego has spent 30+ years helping his clients and employers achieve and exceed their business objectives within roles such as Vice President Operations, General Manager, Lean Facilitator, Business Manager, Senior Program Manager, Plant Manager, Assistant Quality Manager, Process Engineering Manager, and Health & Safety and Environment Manager. Giorgio has directed and guided businesses, designed, led and implemented projects and initiatives resulting in both new annual sales and annual cost savings ranging up to tens and hundreds of thousands, and tens and hundreds of millions, of dollars in Canada, the USA, Mexico, parts of Europe, and East Asia.

In addition to authoring several books and other programs, Giorgio also shares his strategies and ideas as a consultant, coach, mentor, instructor, trainer, and speaker.

Giorgio has been described as an energetic, driven, bottom-line, results-oriented, flexible, pragmatic, *hands-on* problem solver and change agent who is systems-orientated while continuously seeking to eliminate waste. While being a long-term planner, Giorgio is also able to think quickly on his feet, is proactive and able to identify issues and their resolutions using his excellent leadership, communications, negotiation, organizational, analytical, and commercial skills. Throughout his career, Giorgio has been liked and well respected by his clients, employees, employers, customers, suppliers, shareholders, and students.

Giorgio has contributed to, and improved, his clients' and employers' businesses in the areas of leadership, commercial management, profit and loss performance, turnarounds, strategic planning, financial analyses, budgets, organization/systems development, and project management. Giorgio has also designed and led business development, marketing, account management, customer service, supply chain, distribution, and new and innovative product design and development initiatives. Giorgio has extensive experience in, and has led, operations, materials management (order and release management, scheduling, capacity and resource planning, inventory control, procurement, logistics), finance, cost control, quality, production, delivery, engineering, maintenance, facilities, health and safety, environment, human resources, and customer liaison projects. Finally, Giorgio has successfully directed many programs in lean manufacturing, world class manufacturing (WCM), Kaizen, 5S, TPM, VSM, OEE, SMED, cellular manufacturing, one-piece flow, visual management, Kaizen Teian, metrics, ISO 9001/2 & 14001, TS16949, and is familiar with HACCP, GMP concepts and system requirements.

Giorgio has also been described as a focused, confident, and transparent leader who is passionate about improving employee morale, fostering employee empowerment, and creating harmonious business environments under sometimes very challenging circumstances. His unique understanding of human nature, insights, experiences, and extensive people skills have permitted him to dramatically improve an individual's, and groups of individual's, attitudes and motivations to fully contribute to business's successes. With his authentic, open-minded, and innovative approaches, Giorgio has been able to work with all types of people, take charge of challenging situations, and propel businesses and their employees into new and long lasting periods of continuous improvements. Along the way, Giorgio also inspires, teaches, and coaches others to reach their human potential, not only as leaders and employees but as people outside of their work environments.

Contact Giorgio at www.chargeupyourbusinessbook.com   and/or www.gbicego.com for:

- more information, advice, and help with your business and people challenges
- coaching and mentoring needs
- training and instruction requirements
- speaking engagements

# ADDITIONAL RESOURCES

www.chargeupyourbusinessbook.com
www.chargeupyourpeoplebook.com

www.gbicego.com
www.linkedin.com/in/giorgio-bicego-61386111/

www.ingramcontent.com/pod-product-compliance
Lightning Source LLC
Chambersburg PA
CBHW061322220326
41599CB00026B/4995